ILLUSIONS
OF CONTROL

ILLUSIONS OF CONTROL

Striving for Control in Our Personal and Professional Lives

Fathali M. Moghaddam
and Charles Studer

Westport, Connecticut
London

Library of Congress Cataloging-in-Publication Data

Moghaddam, Fathali M.
    Illusions of control : striving for control in our personal and
professional lives / Fathali M. Moghaddam and Charles Studer.
        p.   cm.
    Includes bibliographical references and indexes.
    ISBN 0–275–96025–0 (alk. paper)
    1. Control (Psychology)   I.   Studer, Charles.   II.   Title.
BF611.M63   1998
153.8—dc21   97–43944

British Library Cataloguing in Publication Data is available.

Library of Congress Catalog Card Number: 97–43944
ISBN: 0–275–96025–0

First published in 1998

Praeger Publishers, 88 Post Road West, Westport, CT 06881
An imprint of Greenwood Publishing Group, Inc.

Printed in the United States of America

The paper used in this book complies with the
Permanent Paper Standard issued by the National
Information Standards Organization (Z39.48–1984).

10 9 8 7 6 5 4 3 2 1

Copyright Acknowledgment

All cartoons are reproduced with permission of the artist, A. Kowalski.

Contents

Preface

This book is the result of a fairly unique collaboration between two people with very different experiences and training, but with a shared passion for ideas about how humans construct their world. One of us is a widely published academic psychologist, the other is a "hands on" business manager with over forty years of international experience. The academic psychologist came from the third world and was educated in the West; the business manager came from the West and has spent decades working in third world countries. The third world author studied people in the workplace to test ideas developed in academia, the Western manager came to academia in search of new ideas about culture and behavior. Both writers share a deep interest in the cross-fertilization of the academic and business worlds, and both have been struck by the power that illusions of control exert in the personal and professional lives of people in different societies.

Organization and Style

We have explored illusions of control in both personal and professional domains. The nineteen chapters discuss the historical and evolutionary context of illusions of control, illusions of control in psychological and political life, illusions of control in corporate and organizational life, and illusions of control in economic and cultural life. Thus, the topics covered range from microlevel psychological discussions on "self-control" to macrolevel discussions such as "controlling" inflation, unemployment, and political extremism.

Each chapter begins with an introduction and ends with a brief concluding statement. The main body of each chapter is organized under multiple headings so that chapter sections remain brief. Two critical-thinking exercises follow each chapter, and these can be used for deeper personal reflection and for group discussions.

The message of this book, we feel, is simple and compelling, and we have adopted a direct style to convey this message. Our main concern has been to illuminate new ideas and how they can be of practical use. We have avoided the heavy referencing that is now the norm in most academic publications, because we find this distracts from the main message. Even with this intention, however, we could not avoid providing several hundred references.

Competing Books

When we began our collaboration on this book on illusions of control, we were surprised to find a paucity of publications on this topic. A number of works have been published on related topics, such as *Positive Illusions* (Taylor, 1989) and *Learned Optimism* (Seligman, 1991). A number of books have the term "control" in their titles (e.g., *The Control Revolution*, Beniger, 1986; *Out of Control*, Brzezinski, 1993), but none of these works directly address illusions of control.

Target Audience

This book is primarily intended for students of management, organizational psychology, and social psychology. It would be a suitable supplementary text for a number of courses in these three disciplines. Also, we see it fitting in with the volumes typically found on the bookshelves of managers.

ILLUSIONS
OF CONTROL

1

The Boundaries of Illusions of Control

> Nasrudin was practicing target shooting with a bow and arrow. His first attempt went too far to the right and missed the target completely, and he explained it by saying, `That is how my father used to aim with his bow and arrow.'   On his second attempt, the arrow went too far to the left and again missed the target by a big distance, so he said, `My uncle does it like that.' His third shot fell short and stuck into the ground in front of the target, and he dismissed it by saying, `My brother shoots like this.' Nasrudin's fourth shot hit the bull's eye, and he said triumphantly, `And this is how I hit the target.'

The gambler talking to the dice and willing the numbers to "fall lucky," a mother and a father planning the future of their children, the business manager finalizing a strategic plan for how the company will perform over the next five years, and the government minister announcing steps that will reduce unemployment by half over the next year are all people well known in modern life. What they often have in common is that they all tend to be influenced by *illusions of control*. This involves mistaken beliefs that future changes in personal, social, economic, political, and other domains are under the control of humankind.

As suggested by the ancient Persian story cited at the beginning of the chapter, illusions of control typically arise when people exaggerate the level of control they have over events. Nasrudin, the main character in this and many other stories associated with Sufi teachings, planned to hit the bull's-eye each time he took aim with his bow and arrow. However, his plans did not work out this way on the first three attempts, and in his reconstruction of the event he said each time, that is how his father/uncle/brother shot with a bow and arrow. When his plan did finally work and he hit the bull's-eye, he took credit for the shot and, more importantly, maintained the view that his plan worked once again! Thus, both when he achieved a bull's-eye hit and when he had total misses, he reinterpreted events to make it seem that everything had proceeded according to plan.

At first glance, it may appear that our actions are very different from Nasrudin's, but after closer examination it becomes obvious that there are many instances in everyday life when we act just like him. That is, we carefully draw up plans, just as Nasrudin carefully pulled back on his bow and took aim at the target, but find that during implementation events just do not unfold the way we had expected, and the arrow misses the target. We then proceed to reconstruct the past in a way that preserves the apparent validity of our plans.

The gambler is mistaken in his belief that he can control the dice to "fall lucky"; parents are wrong in thinking they will be able to control the futures of their children; business managers routinely but wrongly assume that they can make their strategic plans come true; and governments are well known for making disastrous mistakes in assuming they can control unemployment and other aspects of national economies.

In this book we explore illusions of control in a variety of domains. Such illusions are a central feature of modern life. They arise in large part because, particularly in Western societies, we are socialized to desire to achieve control, so much so that we construct illusions of control when all the evidence indicates that we lack control. In an era referred to by some as the age of uncertainty, of unreason, and even of chaos, the motivation to try to control events is perhaps inevitable. From control may arise certainty, reason, and order.

The tendency to be influenced by illusions of control is particularly strong in modern western societies, most notably in the United States. The enormous emphasis placed on self-help, individual responsibility, and independence in the United States is associated with a "you can do it if you really try" attitude. Underlying the American dream is a strong theme of the individual person being in control of her or his own destiny, and by implication of surrounding events. This contrasts sharply with a more fatalistic outlook, one involving beliefs in destiny and predetermination, found more often in traditional Eastern cultures.

The Psychological Basis of Illusions of Control

Illusions of control have a psychological basis, and in this sense they involve subjective experiences. The gambler who believes he can beat chance by picking certain favorite numbers in a lottery rather than by being assigned numbers by others (Langer, 1977), or by throwing dice softly for low numbers and harder for high numbers (Henslin, 1967), is acting on a subjective perception of having control over events. Of course, chance will work in the gambler's favor once in a while, and if success comes early then the illusion of control will be even more firmly entrenched. If gamblers start with some wins, then their estimates of their ability to beat the odds become even more inflated, often surviving a long string of losses.

Psychologists have studied the kinds of heuristics, rules of thumb, people use in making estimates about the likelihood of events. For example, people often make errors in their estimations because they are influenced by the ease with which information can be recalled. This availability heuristic means, for example, that although the risk is far higher using car transport, people generally estimate air travel to be riskier (see Fiske & Taylor, 1991). A possible reason for this belief is because airline crashes are far more newsworthy and provide more vivid pictures than do car crashes, they come to mind more readily.

It would be a mistake, however, to conceive of human beings as "thinking machines" who take shortcuts and simply make mistakes in estimation. Our errors of judgment are biased in particular directions, they are not random. The subjective cognitions of people tend to overestimate their degree of control over events, even when, in fact, they have little or no control (Miller & Ross, 1975).

Similarly, human thinking is not divorced from emotions. Cognitions in the real world are very much bound up with emotions and directed toward particular goals. Gone are the days when we thought of human thinking and intelligence as context-independent, abstract entities that exist in isolation. As indicated by the influence of such concepts as emotional intelligence, we now recognize that even intelligence is bound up with emotions and our personal style of social behavior.

In this sense, then, human thinking is goal directed, influenced by emotions, and "hot" and context dependent, rather than "cold" and context independent. In addition to being influenced by context, illusions of control are socially constructed and maintained.

The Social Nature of Illusions of Control

Why is it so difficult to overcome illusions of control? The answer lies in the social nature of illusions of control, the fact that they are shared by groups of individuals who each act to support the shared illusions.

The social and shared nature of illusions of control is often neglected, because the term "illusions" implies thoughts in individual minds. It is tempting to assume that what is "in the mind" is private and dependent on personal rather than social characteristics. The illusions we hold as individuals are social. They evolve through interactions with others, and are maintained and developed though our participation in social life.

For example, the manager is not alone with her five-year plan, she sits on a committee of senior managers. Committee members share ideas about the five-year plan and the control the management hopes to enjoy over the course of future events. There is strong pressure among group members to conform and to help maintain group consensus. As Irving Janis (1972, 1982) showed in his study of groupthink, the tendency for groups to develop and maintain certain illusions of reality can lead to disastrous consequences. An example is the U.S. continuation and escalation of the war in Vietnam during the 1960s and 1970s, in part as a result of illusions of control among the president and his closest group of advisors.

Similar processes underlay the temporary fall of International Business Machines (IBM) in the 1970s and 1980s, from an all-powerful leadership position to that of a giant struggling to survive in a fast-changing environment.

The Pervasive Nature of Illusions of Control

> Reengineering...is the fundamental rethinking and radical redesign of business processes to achieve dramatic improvements in critical, contemporary measures of performance, such as cost, quality, service, and speed.
>
> Hammer & Champy Reengineering the corporation

This is the age of self-control, self-actualization, self-fulfillment, and taking control of our personal, social, and physical universe. The slogan that best captures the spirit of our age might be "take control!"

No wonder buzzwords like "reengineering" have taken over the business world at the turn of the twenty-first century, much as "strategic planning" did in the 1960s. One of the most pervasive features of modern societies is the motivation to control and to construct and nurture illusions of control when actual control fails, as it very often does.

The very language we now use oozes with a feeling of control and joy in control. No longer content to just plan or change, we reengineer! Terms such as "process redesign," "information technology," "business process," "value chain," and "reengineering team" are intended to portray the impression that the environment is being precisely and effectively controlled. It is as if the professionals who achieve such feats know exactly what should be done and who should do what in order to achieve such precision engineering. Typical of this new reengineering ethos is the proposal that the leader appoints the process owner, who convenes a reengineering team to reengineer the process, with assistance from the czar and under the auspices of the steering committee (see Champy, 1995; Hammer & Champy, 1993).

Such language, obviously intended to impress readers with the engineer's power to control change, is a far cry from the actual abilities of managers and their consultants to even understand change, never mind predict and control it.

The Causal Model and Illusions of Control

Illusions of control have a psychological basis, and they also underlie modern psychological science. In other words, not only are illusions of control psychological in nature, but their influence is also important in the way psychologists go about their work, particularly how they develop theories and conduct research. This is a case of the experts being under the influence of the "disease" they study. This disease is the illusion that future events are predictable and controllable, that causes and effects can be identified in linear relationships.

Orthodox psychology, economics, and management science have this very important characteristic in common: adherence to positivism and a "causal" model of science. They believe that events in psychological, social, and other domains have causes, and that the job of the social scientist is to identify such causes in order to establish causal relations (see Moghaddam & Harré, 1995). Thus, for example, psychologists look for causal relations between attitudes and behavior, and economists do so between the unemployment level and inflation. The business strategist uses such "facts" about causal relations, together with data about the business environment, to draw up strategic plans for how the corporation will perform over the next five years.

In the real world, however, an event is influenced by multitudes of ever-changing patterns of other events, and causal relations very seldom work out according to the models of orthodox psychology, economics, or management science. Traditional models depict behavior in linear terms, but the true relationship is nonlinear. David Parker and Ralph Stacey (1994) have succinctly highlighted this difference. In a linear relationship, each cause has one effect, but in a nonlinear relationship, a cause can have multiple effects. In linear relationships the whole is the sum of its parts. If you break down the whole into parts, you do not lose anything. In nonlinear relationships, the whole is more than the sum of its parts.

Gestalt psychologists tried to introduce the idea of nonlinear relationships into psychology and other social sciences early in the twentieth century. They had very little success. Since the 1970s, the concept of nonlinear relationships has been pushed by supporters of the chaos theory, but again with little impact on the mainstream social sciences.

The dominant approach in psychology, and social sciences generally, continues to be linear models of behavior. The search for simple cause-effect relationships continues. This approach is convenient, but ineffective. Such causal models are characterized by a failure to predict actual events. Despite this situation, we do not find the psychologists packing their bags, the economists abandoning the World Bank and the IMF, or the business managers giving up their model building and strategic plans at corporate headquarters. Their illusions of control keep them going along the same path.

Of course, we should not be so harsh on the professionals. After all, we do the very same thing in our everyday lives. Each year, for example, millions of us convince ourselves that we shall exert self-control and stick to a newly devised and expensively purchased diet plan to lose those extra pounds. After a month or two, we fail to lose weight and seem to forget about the experience altogether, only to start again with a new "improved" diet plan, all the while being under the illusion that we are in control (for a broader discussion on weight loss, see Logue, 1991).

The factors influencing weight are about 60 percent environmental and 40 percent inherited. Even if we were 80 percent successful in controlling environmental factors, we would still only achieve less than 50 percent success rate. Thus, even in the best of circumstances, the belief that you have taken control of your weight is illusory.

The Good, the Bad, and the Ugly of Illusions

The term "illusions" tends to have negative connotations in Western societies, and in the United States in particular. It implies that a viewpoint is at a distance from reality, that it is mistaken and dysfunctional. It is common for us to talk about "suffering" from an illusion, but it is rather rare to mention possible benefits of illusions.

It would be a grave mistake, however, to assume that illusions of control are always bad. Such illusions probably play a very constructive role in much of our personal lives, particularly because they help us maintain a positive and optimistic outlook, even in the face of defeat. Anyone who has ever done poorly on a test, or been ridiculed by friends, or been turned down for a promotion at work, or suffered a broken heart at the hands of some beautiful but unreachable loved one (only one of the authors of this book has had this last problem) knows firsthand about the constructive and supportive functions of illusions. The power and value of holding positive illusions have been thoroughly documented by psychologists (Seligman, 1991; Taylor, 1989).

We sometimes cope with our failures by holding illusions of no control. A driver may explain away his part in an accident by saying, "It was out of my hands, the road was slippery and the other cars were going too fast." A student may justify her failure to complete a project on time by blaming high-tech equipment, "My paper is complete, but the computer will not print it out." This attribution of the causes of negative events to factors external to ourselves has become well known through the work of psychologists.

Of more interest to us are the very common situations where we maintain illusions of control, and even reconstruct events so that our control in a "failure" situation reflects on us positively rather than negatively. We often have illusions about our control of future events. For example, a manager will say, "The discovery and launch of the new product will take place in four phases and be completed in five years at a cost of $120 million." When things do not turn out as we had planned, we reconstruct the past and rearrange our plans so as to maintain our illusions of control. The same manager might then respond, "The plan was, of course, adjusted and finetuned, and everything worked out well in the end. The new product was launched in eight years at a cost of $350 million." Anyone who is familiar with the history of real projects, from the internationally known ones like the Channel tunnel, the Concord aircraft, the Sydney Opera House, to the small projects involving our own little offices and homes, immediately identify with this situation.

When Are Illusions of Control Harmful?

We have noted that illusions of control can be beneficial, giving individuals the means to feel good about themselves and their roles in both positive and negative events. However, there is also an "ugly" side to illusions of control.

The ugly aspect of illusions of control arises when illusions lead us so far away from practical reality that our very survival, as individuals, as business organizations, as nations, as one of nature's species, is seriously threatened. The gambler who continues to gamble until all of his money is lost, always believing that he can make the dice fall right, the business manager who refuses to recognize that events have overtaken the company's strategic plan, and the government minister who fails to accept that his policies have not brought inflation under control are all involved in situations where the gap between perceptions and reality can lead to disaster, for the individual, the corporation, or even the nation.

The Orientation and Plan of this Book

Our orientation is diagnostic, and our main goal is to identify and highlight illusions of control. We do not think it useful, at this stage, to propose detailed recipes for coping with illusions of control in all the many practical domains that they influence. Guided by the idea that the most practical solutions arise out of the best theoretical formulations, we believe that our diagnostic approach is a constructive step toward effective solutions, that will be developed by practitioners in their own domains.

Our discussions lead to a broad general proposal, captured in the following motto: long-term vision, short-term goals and strategies. We believe it is useful to adopt general long-term goals as a means of directing energies and mobilizing resources. However, practical strategies must be short term so as to maintain the highest level of flexibility with respect to how we get to our goals. Just as important in this process is the explicit formulation of assumptions underlying the adopted goals and strategies. Whether we are attempting to bring about change through clinical therapy, counseling, corporate leadership, or motherly advice in a family, we can best avoid the pitfalls of illusions of control when our assumptions are made explicitly.

The nineteen chapters of this book explore illusions of control in a wide variety of domains, from the psychological level of the individual psyche to macro societal levels. The chapters deal with a wide range of issues on the theme of control, including historical and evolutionary background to illusions of control, psychological and political aspects of illusions of control, illusions of control in organizational and business life, as well as in cultural and economic spheres.

Our concern is not just to highlight illusions of control in everyday "lay" life, but also to identify and assess illusions of control in the professional lives of psychologists, economists, and management researchers. At the most basic level, psychologists, economists, and management researchers are all concerned with human behavior. They all study what people do and have developed elaborate models to explain what causes people to behave the way they do. Such models are based on assumptions, but it is often difficult to identify these assumptions because they are buried under mountains of mathematical and statistical formulas, terminology, and sometimes even jargon.

Concluding Comment

Part of what it means to be an advanced society includes the achievement of greater control over both human and environmental domains. We need to reassess the assumption that science can lead to the discovery of causes of events and thus to ways of controlling causal relations. Much of what happens in the world is not explained by cause-effect relations, and the idea of control though such relations is illusory.

Critical Thinking Exercises

(1) What are illusions of control and are they necessarily bad?
(2) What is a causal model in the social sciences?

2

The Emergence of Modern
Illusions of Control

...I have bedimmed
The noontide sun, called forth the mutinous winds,
And 'twixt the green sea and the azured vault
Set roaring war; to the dread rattling thunder
Have I given fire, and rifted Jove's stout oak
With his own bolt; the strong-based promontory
Have I made shake, and by the spurs plucked up
The pine and cedar. Graves at my command
Have waked their sleepers, oped, and let 'em forth
By my so potent art.

Shakespeare, The Tempest (V.1.lines 41-50)

When Shakespeare (1564-1616) wrote these lines over four centuries ago, there
was already a fundamental change underway in Western thinking about human
control and the relationship of people to the world around them. These changes in
worldview involved an attempt to develop a science for the purpose of controlling
nature. They also were associated with the erosion and threatened disappearance
of humankind's central and absolute position in the universe. These two themes in
historical development went hand in hand but brought about conflicting outcomes.

The newly emerging sciences allowed humans to better control their world, as
reflected, for example, in the practical changes brought about by steam power and
the railways. These improvements were associated with the new belief that the
world would eventually be controlled through science. The new sciences were
accompanied by the collapse of traditional views of the position and role of human
beings in the universe. Thus, the modern human experience has been inherently

contradictory, involving both greater control and less certainty; a greater feeling of attaining power and a growing feeling of being purposeless; an increased capacity to make and direct change but a loss of direction and purpose.

It is with this historic contradiction in mind that we can better appreciate the emergence of illusions of control, which are in large part designed to derive certainty through control.

It is telling that the Shakespearian character who expressed these lines (at the beginning of the chapter) was a magician/scientist, Prospero, the former duke of Milan. Prospero's art may seem fantastic and his claims unlikely, but they are in accord with a much wider intellectual movement aimed at understanding nature in order to control its forces.

Science as Greater Control

This intellectual movement was generally foreshadowed by the Renaissance and the scientific methods of Leonardo Da Vinci (1452-1519), among others. For example, Leonardo's artistic creations were based on a very detailed and direct study of nature. His engineering and architectural designs clearly demonstrate his empirical approach to understanding the world. By the mid-sixteenth century, the importance of empirical methods was widely accepted. This is reflected in the writings of Francis Bacon (1561-1626) on scientific method and the research of Galileo (1564-1642), which sought proof of the Copernican theory. Indeed, if we need a specific benchmark as the start of modern science, the best is probably Nicholas Copernicus's (1473-1543) rationalization of the Ptolemaic cosmology, which places the sun at the center of the universe, with the earth moving around it in an annual revolution, and the earth rotating on its axis every twenty-four hours.

Science and the "Loss" of Human Identity

Copernican theory did away with the explanation of night and day that assumed the sun and the planets revolved around the earth each day. But this "doing away" was also symbolic of a much more socially and politically significant shift, involving a move away from the orthodox church. According to Holy Scripture, Joshua ordered the sun, not the earth, to stand still. The attempt by church authorities, both Catholic and Protestant, to dismiss the Copernican view as an absurdity during the sexteenth century came to collision course during the seventeenth century, as symbolized by the persecution of Galileo and his forced capitulation (even "reformers" such as Martin Luther [1483-1546] were hostile to the Copernican model). The seeds of experimental science had been sown and the harvest was inevitable, culminating in the works of Isaac Newton (1642-1727) in the eighteenth century and Charles Darwin (1809-1882) in the nineteenth century.

Whereas the Copernican model replaced the earth as the center of the physical universe, Darwinian theory replaced humans as the center of the biological universe. During that period of orthodoxy in the West, the major religions still had a monopoly over the worldview (as is still very much the case in many developing societies), and they conceived of humans as unique, completely separate from the animal world. According to evolution theory, however, humans are on a continuum with all other biological beings and share the same ancestry with them, an idea that led critics such as Bishop Samuel Wilberforce (1805-1873) to ask whether it was from his maternal or paternal lineage that Darwin was descended from the apes. This brought about a retort from Thomas Huxley (1825-1895), "Darwin's bulldog," that he would rather be descended from an ape than a bishop (see Dennett, 1995).

Economic Control

The revolutions taking place in the physical and natural sciences from the sixteenth to the nineteenth centuries were matched by revolutions in economics, politics, and the social sciences generally. The major breakthrough in the realm of political economics came with the work of the Scottish economist Adam Smith (1723-1790). Smith is often regarded as the father of capitalism and contrasted with Karl Marx (1818-1883). If he is the father of capitalism, it is not because of the sentiments he expressed. A careful reading of *The Wealth of Nations* (Smith, 1776/1976), as well as his other writings that deal more directly with moral philosophy, reveals that he was in many ways more sympathetic to the plight of the underdog than the capitalist class. However, in so far as he advocated a free market economy with as little interference as possible from government, the title of "father of capitalism" is aptly his.

Specialization and the Greater Need for Managerial Planning

Although Smith advocated that the best government is the one that governs least, his ideas concerning divisions of labor and economic life more generally inevitably make economic planning and control a central activity in society. This is because, as he points out himself, increased divisions of labor lead to a situation where each person produces a narrower and narrower kind of product. The result is that people need to rely more and more on exchange in order to acquire goods. In addition, individuals and organizations need to be able to compete successfully in the "free market." Thus, there needs to be effective planning for keeping stock, predicting future supply and demand, and making efficient use of resources in order to survive in the market. All this points to a greater need for predicting and controlling economic events.

Within the organization, increased specialization leads to a greater need for managerial control. As employees, departments, and divisions become more and more specialized, there is a greater danger of fragmentation within the organization. Fewer and fewer people in the organization have an understanding of what other employees are doing, and where they themselves fit in "the big

picture." To combat this danger, additional levels of management are introduced to coordinate the efforts of increasingly specialized units. In the automotive industry, there are now twelve levels of command between the chief executive officer and the factory worker assembling the car and the salesperson persuading customers to buy it. Thus, the perceived need for managerial control, and the levels of management involved, rises with increased specialization (see Moghaddam, 1997, ch.4).

The fruits of such concerns are clearly evident in strategic planning and other managerial activities intended to give managers a higher degree of control. As we shall see in the chapters ahead, much of this "managerial control" is illusory.

Marx and "Central" Control

If planning and control were an unintended but inevitable concern of those following the ideas of Smith, David Ricardo (1772-1823), and other classic economists, they were an explicitly intended concern of Karl Marx's political economy. Marx's model involved a peculiar mixture of the inevitable and the planned in human history. He proposed that human societies evolve along predictable and lawful paths, so that capitalism must collapse with the achievement of class consciousness among the proletariate. From the resulting proletariate revolution would arise a dictatorship of the proletariate, and eventually a classless society that had no need for a government. In one sense, then, the inevitability of these developments seem to make planning and control less important.

In another sense, however, Marx's model gave central place to planning and control because the revolutionary changes he foresaw were always conditional upon certain circumstances being achieved through effective manipulation of the world. The revolutions he predicted would not just come about, they would be brought about in large part by the leadership and management of a progressive vanguard. More specifically, for example, the move from a dictatorship of the proletariate to a classless society could only be achieved through thorough development and diligent execution of effective plans, or there would be "regression" instead of "progression" in social evolution.

That a Marxist perspective leads to attempts to strictly control and manage all aspects of society is clearly evident from the experiences of the former USSR and other Eastern Bloc countries, as well as China, Cuba, and other surviving communist states. It is also evident, but to a lesser extent, in the policies of socialist governments that have come to power in Western societies.

Just as it is self-evident that Marxist models lead to serious attempts at absolute control through central powers, experience shows that such control is truly illusory. The collapse of communist systems one after another testifies to this fact.

Psychology: The Ultimate Illusion of Understanding and Control

The mid-nineteenth century saw the birth of modern psychology, perhaps the most audacious, and some would say outrageous, systematized form of illusion of control. If we want to select an exact starting date for this enfant terrible, the best one is traditionally taken to be 1879, when the German psychologist Wilhelm Wundt (1832-1920) established the first formal psychology laboratory at the University of Leipzig. Wundt envisaged two fundamentally different agendas for the new science, and it is rather telling that only one of these agendas has been taken up by modern psychologists. As we shall see, this very choice reflects a grand form of illusion of control (see Robinson, 1995).

Wundt's first "high control" agenda was for a laboratory-based science to study memory, perception, and other aspects of individual psychological functioning. In many ways this was a science of human capabilities, best exemplified by the work of Hermann Ebbinghaus (1850-1908) on memory: how individuals memorize, retain, recall, and forget information over time. Using himself as the main participant in his research, Ebbinghaus demonstrated a number of ways in which human memory has limited capabilities, such as limits in short-term memory. He was also the first to use *nonsense syllables*, two consonants with a vowel in between that do not form a word, such as "zil" and "kif." Nonsense syllables are assumed to serve as relatively meaningless items in memory research, and thus enhance the control achieved by researchers.

The experimental laboratory method allows the experimenter to exert a high degree of control because all the factors in a laboratory (such as the level of meaning of items in a memory study) can be effectively controlled. By varying one factor (referred to as the "independent variable") and testing the effect of this variation on some other factor (the "dependent variable"), and by keeping all other factors in the laboratory situation constant, it is possible to identify causal relations (see Moghaddam, 1998).

For example, if person A learns a series of phrases and then forgets them over time, we know that relearning the same series will require less trials for that person than for person B who is exposed to the series for the first time. This can be established by comparing the performance of person A (the relearner) and person B (the first-time learner) under identical conditions. The superior performance of person A allows us to conclude that the initial learning experience caused the relearning to require fewer trials.

Psychology as the science of understanding, prediction, and control of behavior developed out of Wundt's first agenda for the new science. The culmination of this approach in the first half of the twentieth century was behaviorism, in particular B. F. Skinner's brand of this school of thought, while its zenith in the second half of the twentieth century was cognitive psychology.

The Cognitive Revolution and Control

At first glance it may appear that modern cognitive psychology has little in common with Skinner's behaviorism. Today's students of psychology are taught that behaviorism failed because it neglected the mind, the self, and consciousness in general, and attempted to account for behavior simply through the "laws of learning" that were supposed to explain all stimulus-response (S-R) associations. Some even see behaviorism as "evil" because the ideal society depicted by Skinner (1948) in his *Walden Two* allows little room for traditional human ideals of freedom and dignity.

Cognitive psychology, it is claimed, is fundamentally different from behaviorism because it focuses on thought processes. The cognitive revolution allowed for the return of the mind, the self, and other topics associated with human consciousness. However, this traditional description of the relationship between behaviorism and cognitive psychology fails to take a number of things into consideration.

Although behaviorism and cognitive psychology differ in many ways, they share the fundamental characteristic of assuming that human behavior can best be explained by a causal model (Moghaddam & Studer, 1997). "Causes" are discovered in stimulus-response relations in the case of behaviorism, and in cognitive processes in the case of cognitive psychology. For both behaviorism and cognitive psychology, the laboratory method dominantes because it is most compatible with the causal model. Consequently, modern cognitive psychology studies social behavior by isolating individuals in the laboratory context, with the purpose of discovering the cognitive processes that act as "causal mechanisms" in behavior. In this way, modern psychology has extended Wundt's first agenda for the study of topics such as memory to also cover the study of social relations.

Wundt's Second Agenda

But for Wundt the "causal" model used to study memory performance and the like was totally inadequate for understanding, let alone predicting and controlling, social relations. Wundt had a second "no control" agenda for psychology, one concerned with "folk psychology," but this has been totally ignored by modern psychologists. He believed that social relations should be studied through examining cultural characteristics, including language, mythologies, and social beliefs, and that this could only be achieved outside the laboratory.

Why has modern psychology neglected Wundt's second agenda? Why have modern researchers, against Wundt's advice, preferred to study social relations in the laboratory? Why has modern social psychology concerned itself almost exclusively with the study of white middle-class college students in laboratory settings? The major reason, we believe, is that modern psychologists are motivated to maintain an illusion of control. As long as they restrict themselves to the study of short-term "social" episodes involving students in the laboratory setting, they can maintain the illusion that they can understand, predict, and even to some degree control behavior.

Concluding Comment

Enormous scientific progress has been made during the last five hundred years, particularly in the physical and biological sciences. The outcome, however, has not been increased control in all domains. Knowledge in biology, chemistry, mathematics, physics, and so on has allowed us to achieve vast industrial output. We now have more goods and services than at any other time in history. Unfortunately, the same "control" has resulted in global warming and possibly other as yet undetected problems that are not under control. In the social sciences, similarly, we are able to control the small, the minor, by isolating bits of behavior. Our measurements and observations in the confines of laboratories or within the limits of our computer simulations have given rise to the illusion that we can predict and control human behavior in the world outside the laboratory.

Critical Thinking Exercises

(1) In what way is scientific progress associated with both a change in human identity and a greater sense of control?
(2) In what ways are both behaviorism and cognitive psychology concerned with control?

3

Evolution, Runaway Selection, and Control

"That's how we survived," the archaeologist was explaining. One of the authors of this book had volunteered to work on an archaeological dig in Scotland and was now being shown the main dig area by the research director.

"Humans have always been motivated to master the environment, to change and shape the land. That's how we survived." The archaeologist was pointing to a large clearing made by his Scottish ancestors over a thousand years ago.

"Think of all the effort they put into this." It was an awe-inspiring sight that underlined his point. These people had tried to shape their physical environment in major ways, using only their primitive tools and bare hands.

The idea that humans should be motivated to actually control their own environments makes a lot of sense from the point's of view of evolutionary theory, and functionalist perspectives in general. Evidence from the earliest eras of human history suggests that the ability of homo sapiens to alter the environment, to adapt it to their needs rather than to always adapt themselves to local ecologies, was crucial to survival and progress. This ability allowed us to influence our own evolution in some ways. Of course, because we only achieved limited control of the environment, we never escaped the grip of competition for survival. Throughout human history, part of the population has survived while other parts have perished.

Charles Darwin (1809-1888) and Alfred Wallace (1823-1913), the co-founders of evolutionary theory, were both influenced in very important ways by the historical "population" essay written by Thomas Malthus (1766-1834) in the late eighteenth century. Malthus's thesis was simple enough: food production increases arithmetically (e.g., 1, 2, 3, 4), while population increases geometrically (e.g., 1,

2, 4, 8), with the result that there is always competition between people for scarce food, and thus cycles of famine and relative abundance occur. Both Darwin and Wallace came away from this essay with an important idea: In the competition for survival, some individuals are "advantaged" and are more likely to survive. For example, some individuals are faster and more effective at evading predators, or are better able to cope with extreme temperature changes, or have longer necks and have better access to food in higher places. In short, they are "fitter" and do best in the race for survival. Herbert Spencer (1820-1903) introduced the term "survival of the fittest," and then later the notion of "ecological fitness" became popular (for a review of history of ideas in biology, see Mayr, 1982).

The concept of "fitness" only makes sense in relation to a particular ecology. For example, people who thrive on Wall Street have adapted to the particular needs of that very peculiar jungle; they may not thrive if we transport them to the jungles of Brazil. Similarly, the Yanomamo are a people adapted for survival in the northern Brazilian jungles (Chagnon, 1988, 1992), and they would not find the Wall Street jungle very hospitable (for that matter, even some Europeans and Americans might prefer the jungles of Brazil to those of Wall Street).

It is meaningless to ask, Who is better suited to survive? without also considering the kind of ecological conditions in which they would have to survive. A cat is very well adapted for the life conditions of a cat, but would not do at all well if it encountered the life conditions of a mouse. The American professional politician is well adapted for the cutthroat life of party politics on Capitol Hill, but may not survive the cutthroat existence experienced by drug pushers in downtown Washington D.C. (for that matter, drug pushers might find it even tougher to survive Washington politics than the inner-city jungle). Each has adapted to a particular ecology and gained some control over events in his or her particular life.

The evolutionary perspective leads us to question the function of things: What is the function of "control" in human survival? Actual control of the environment obviously has a key function, because by altering the environment humans can directly change the very requirements for survival and thus improve or diminish their own chances for survival. For example, the buildings we construct enable us to live in even the most harsh climates, in the Arctic, in the Sahara, under the sea, or even in outer space. Of course, not all of the ways in which we change the environment necessarily improve our chances for survival. For example, environmental pollution has many adverse side effects, such as depletion of the ozone layer, which may decrease our chances for survival.

The "advanced" industrial nations have become particularly effective at controlling the environment. They are capable of transforming the environment on a massive scale in a fairly short amount of time, building long roads, constructing massive dams, creating huge cities even in hostile climates. In a sense, the level of control achieved by a society is a good indicator of the level of economic progress made. The developed nations are advanced in science and industry and enjoy a high level of control, whereas the underdeveloped countries have primitive sciences and industries, and thus have far less control.

In the very long term, the survival of homo sapiens may depend just as much on how they adapt the environment, on earth or perhaps on other planets, to their own survival needs as how they adapt themselves to the environment. Obviously, then, the actual control humans achieve is vital to their survival, or so it seems.

Is Control Necessarily Functional?

One of the most spectacular sights nature has to offer is that of a peacock displaying its feathers. The male typically tries to position itself so that it will be visible in full plumage to the female. This magnificent display of color, with the male stretching and strutting to its greatest advantage, is as risky as it is spectacular.

In the short term, this fantastic display is risky because it is easy for predators to sneak up behind the outstretched tail of a displaying peacock. This immediate risk is multiplied many times in the long term by the additional dangers the peacock has to face because of the vulnerable position in which it is placed by its beautiful feathers. Like other birds with extravagant feathers, the peacock is handicapped in its movements by that which makes its beautiful to the female. The case of the peacock is one of many where evolution seems to have created a handicap with which an organism must deal.

In answer to the question, Why do peacocks have such elaborate tails?" Darwin responded simply that females prefer such displays. This answer, however, did not satisfy some thinkers, who searched for more clues to explain this kind of apparently paradoxical situation.

Cases involving "handicaps" and other forms of "dysfunctional" characteristics that continue to survive over evolutionary cycles are of enormous theoretical importance. They demonstrate that in order for a characteristic of an organism to survive, the characteristic does not need to be functional. This raises another question: How do we explain the survival of characteristics that are not functional? Darwin's explanation that peacocks have fancy feathers because peahens prefer fancy feathers is unsatisfactory, but has it been replaced by a better explanation? Fortunately, we can maintain our construction of "science as progress" by saying we now do have better explanations.

One such explanation was offered by the innovative English geneticist Ronald Fisher (1890-1962), and it goes a long way toward solving some of the mystery. At first glance, Fisher's explanation also seems circular. Females prefer fancy feathers, because females prefer fancy feathers. By this he meant that any female who "flouts fashion" and mates with peacocks that do not have fancy feathers will have sons without fancy feathers who will be ignored by other females. This seemingly simplistic idea has found considerable support from work on mathematical modeling.

Research following Fisher's model supports the idea that evolution can be

dictated by "fashion" rather than functional adaptation. In certain conditions, what may start as a random preference takes on a life of its own and grows into a pattern of "runaway evolution."

Survival in the Business World

> "In my business, life is like a jungle. It's the strong who survive, the weak get eaten up. You have to be among the leaders, or you fall behind and become their victims."

The person who expressed this view to one of us during a recent interview is a senior manager in a New York advertising firm, but this basic idea is commonly held by managers in many different businesses. That business involves the "survival of the fittest" is a pervasive belief. One of the first implications of this belief seems to be that what survives is necessarily more functional. If business A survives and business B does not, then presumably business A serves some purpose, is "needed" in some way, whereas business B is not needed by the market to the same degree.

Can we then conclude that business A is better than business B? We can, if we clarify that "better" simply means being more effective within the present economic circumstances. If circumstances change, then business B might become better. Furthermore, we cannot assume that the goods business A produces are better; only that they meet demand. It may be that business B produces a better product, for which there is insufficient demand (consider an artist who is not recognized for her genius during her own lifetime, and is only recognized centuries later).

Concluding Comment

We have argued that in order for a phenomenon to survive, it does not necessarily have to be functional although many things that survive are functional in a limited sense. They are "better" in the sense that they meet the demands of prevailing environmental conditions. Our proposition is that illusions of control are functional because they help humans better meet environmental demands. The illusion that you have control over different aspects of your life enables you to enjoy peace of mind.

Critical Thinking Exercises

(1) Evolutionary theory leads to the conclusion that whatever survives is superior. Do you agree? What does "superior" mean here?
(2) What kinds of functions could be served by illusions of control?

4

Self-Control: Psychological Control at the Personal Level

Out, damned spot! out, I say! One; two:
why then, `tis time to do't. Hell is murky!
Fie, my lord, fie! a soldier, and afeard?

Shakespeare, *Macbeth* (V. i)

As the plot unravels around the murderous husband and wife team in Shakespeare's play *Macbeth*, Lady Macbeth loses her mind. Having successfully plotted with her husband to kill the king, the bloodshed and intrigues that follow prove too much for her. In an extreme sense, she loses control.

At the other extreme, we have in *Hamlet* an example of complete self-control in the most demanding circumstance. Lady Macbeth imagines she sees spots of blood on her hands and clothes, but the ghost that Hamlet sees is not supposed to be imaginary. Hamlet is led to the ghost by others, and then hears the ghost speak to him directly: "Adieu, adieu, adieu! remember me," Shakespeare, *Hamlet* (I. v).

With this mournful plea, the ghost of Hamlets's father, the assassinated king, leaves the stage in Shakespeare's great tragedy, *Hamlet, Prince of Denmark*. Following this apparition, Hamlet declares his resolution to sweep all other concerns and thoughts aside, and to single-mindedly pursue the revenge of his assassinated father. Throughout the rest of the play, Hamlet demonstrates heroic control of himself, channeling all of his energies toward exposing the main assassin, his uncle. Nothing can stand between Hamlet and his duty to revenge his father, not the love of the beautiful Ophelia, who might have become his bride, nor the love of his mother, who is now married to his uncle.

Hamlet does bring the assassins to justice, but at the cost of his own life. This represents an extreme form of "self-control," which is a major preoccupation in the socialization of children in Western societies. Children are seen to be more mature and well developed if they are able to forego an immediate reward in order to obtain a greater reward later.

The motivation to achieve self-control is so strongly instilled during childhood that it directs much of adult behavior. Thus, "being in control of oneself" is assumed to be a basic prerequisite to healthy adult life. Often, however, such control is illusory, in the sense that it is imagined rather than actual. Nonetheless, people prefer to hold illusions of control about themselves, rather than believe they lack self-control.

The Fall and Rise of the Self as Object

The control of the self involves much more than delay or denial of gratification. Another major concern of self-control is associated with self-actualization or self-growth. The humanistic psychologists, particularly Carl Rogers (1961) and Abraham Maslow (1970), are to a large extent responsible for popularizing the emphasis on self growth in the latter part of the twentieth century. Growth of the "self" has come to be seen as part of a healthy development.

Another factor associated with the focus on the self since the 1960s is the decline of behavioristic psychology. A central tenet of behaviorism is that in order to become a true science, psychology must only be concerned with what is objectively measurable: that is, observable behavior. This means that metaphysical concepts such as the "self" must be set aside because they can not be observed and measured directly (see Hearnshaw, 1987, for a review of the history of Western psychology).

It is fashionable today to dismiss behaviorism as simplistic, even foolish, and to forget that J. B. Watson's 1913 "behaviorist manifesto" came like a breath of fresh air because it seemed to sweep away all the cobwebs and clear the way for a true science of behavior (see Watson, 1930). There would be no more reliance on reported mental lives, because such things could not be directly measured. Only the directly observable would be included in psychological science. Psychology would become like the "hard" sciences, such as chemistry and physics, and only deal with the objective world.

Do chemists ever ask enzymes why they behave as they do? Do physicists even talk to atoms? Why should psychologists talk to their objects of study? The only way forward was to simply copy the other sciences and report the objectively verifiable.

Parallel to these trends in psychology, economists, sociologists, and other social scientists were also developing their disciplines as "sciences of cause and effect." They, too, were becoming increasingly focused on objectively establishing cause-effect relations, particularly to explain inflation, employment, and other aspects of the larger picture.

Behaviorism and the American Dream

The promise that behaviorism would become a truly objective science was one reason for the rapid spread of this new creed. Another very critical factor was the match between behaviorism and the meritocracy ideology that in theory at least has dominated in the United States.

From its inception, behaviorism has been a peculiarly American enterprise. Although many behaviorist ideas have their roots in the work of Europeans, such as Ivan Pavlov (1849-1936), they have taken on uniquely American characteristics. Most important behaviorism matched the ideology of the American dream and meritocracy. It is the environment, behaviorists argued, that shapes people. The critical factor in life is not our biological makeup, but our environmental shaping. We can make anything of anybody. Give me a child, the behaviorist pioneer Watson declared, and I shall shape him or her into the adult you desire, a doctor, waiter, lawyer, shopkeeper, whatever. This ideology implied that we all start with the same possibilities, and that where we end up in the social system is not predetermined by biology.

This "open possibilities" behaviorist idealogy was a good fit with the American dream, according to which the United States is a land of open opportunities, where it is possible for anyone to make it up the social hierarchy. It is not the position into which one is born, one's starting place, but the personal qualities that one develops that matter.

As far as behaviorism implied an open system, then, it matched the aspirations of American society. However, when Skinner went on to argue for a need to set up the technology for "social engineering" that would seriously shape people, this seemed to many Americans to be "un-American" in its limitations of personal freedom.

Thus, behaviorism matched the American dream in so far as it endorsed the idea of everyone starting "from the same place" and with the same advantages, but it conflicted with the American dream in that it focused on "environmental shaping" rather than "personal motivation" as the driving force behind individual progress. It was when Skinner argued for setting aside "outdated" ideals such as "freedom and dignity," the very individual freedom and personal dignity that Americans cherish, at least in theory, that behaviorism was pushed to the sidelines (Skinner, 1971). Humanistic and cognitive psychologies took over from behaviorism in the 1960s, bringing back the self to mainstream academic life in the United States and in other Western societies.

Half a Century Later, Still Confused about the Self

Go to any magazine stand in the United States, and you will be confronted by hundreds of articles, even whole magazines, that focus on the "self." Self-improvement programs are announced hourly on TV and radio stations. The self has become central to Western, and particularly American, lives. It is not just members of the "me generation" who are preoccupied with the self: we have all become obsessive about the self.

The rise of concern for the self in popular culture has coincided with the resurrection of the self in academic discourse. The self is once again a respectable topic in academia, as reflected by the hundreds of publications that have appeared on this topic since the 1970s.

Two things are clear about the treatment of the self in modern writings. First, control is a major concern. The exploration of the self is driven by a concern to direct our inner experiences, usually toward "growth" or "actualization" or some other idealized state identified by gurus such as Rogers and Maslow. In many cases, the desire for control is explicitly stated. For example, in most kinds of psychological therapy, including the various shades of psychodynamic and humanistic therapies, some form of control is attempted so that change of inner life can be brought about.

A second feature of the diverse modern writings on the self is that they are still struggling to clear up basic questions, such as whether or not the self is unitary. Writers sometimes seem to provide varying accounts simply because they are talking about very different conceptions of the self. The term "self" is sometimes used when something else is meant. So, before we turn to the issue of self-control, we need to make clear what exactly is meant by the term "self."

The Structure of the Self: The "I" and the "Me"

When you read this sentence, you are capable of reflecting on yourself. A traditional distinction between an "I" and a "me" helps to clarify this reflexive ability humans possess. The I is a narrator, telling a story about a me, which serves as the object of narration. The I seems to stand apart from the action, while the me is the actor engaged in the action.

The I/me distinction, with the I as narrator and the me as the object of the narration, is evident in the writings of some novelists of note. For example, Charles Dickens starts his marvelous tale *David Copperfield* by making use of this distinction. The story begins with the narrator recounting episodes in the experiences of the me:

> Whether I shall turn out to be the hero of my own life, or whether that
> station will be held by anybody else, these pages must show. To begin

> my life with the beginning of my life, I record that I was born (as I have
> been informed and believe) on a Friday, at twelve o'clock at night. It
> was remarked that the clock began to strike, and I began to cry,
> simultaneously.

As David Copperfield recounts his tale, "my life," it is the I talking about the me. But in addition to talking about the me from the perspective of the I, David Copperfield is able to talk about the me from the perspective of other persons in his life story. This strategy of telling the story of the same character from the perspective of different persons is found in even a more refined form in what has been termed the "polyphonic novel," such as the works of Dostoyevsky (Tan & Moghaddam, 1995).

Similarly, in our everyday lives we are capable of holding conversations "within ourselves," involving the voices of many imagined characters. For example, a person coming home very late and very drunk may think ahead to the scene awaiting at home and the conversation that will ensue with a spouse, a mother-in-law, or the children. Each of the "other voices" will see the me from a particular perspective. For example, the mother-in-law may be less forgiving than the spouse (this is certainly the case for one of the authors).

In Dickens's story, the David Copperfield known to the various characters is to some extent different. For example, his mother and stepfather know very different David Copperfields, just as we in our lives are seen as "different selves" by our work colleagues, our parents, our spouses, our children, our banker, our car agent, and so on. This led William James to conclude that each of us has as many "social selves" as there are people who know us.

Wrong Conclusions about the Self

A focus on "multiple voices" within the self seems to imply that there are multiple selves.

At the very least, the I/me distinction seems to imply that there are two selves, or how could persons talk about themselves? Must there not be a narrator and an object of narration, two separate entities, in order for a story to be told?

This line of reasoning leads us to the wrong conclusions, and we realize this when we take a critical look at the relationship between the language we use and reality we assume.

One of the most valuable lessons passed on to us by Ludwig Wittgenstein, probably the most original philosopher of the twentieth century, is that we should not assume the characteristics of the world from the language that we use to describe phenomena. Language serves a useful communication function, but just because we communicate ideas about the world through language does not mean that that language accurately reflects the world. In the case of the self, just because we find it useful to describe the experiences of ourselves by using such terms as "I" and "me" should not lead us to assume that these entities actually exist as separate selves.

The Unitary Self

A first step toward recognizing the unitary nature of the self is to distinguish between self, personal identity, self-identity and social self. Self refers to the sense of being, the basic feeling of consciousness that all humans experience. Personal identity encompasses those characteristics that serve to identify an individual and could be used as official markers. A person's name, birth certificate, passport number, social security number, fingerprints, and the like would all be part of personal identity. Self-identity, on the other hand, comprises all the autobiographical information a person possesses, including all the personal and intimate experiences unique to this one individual. Finally, social self is concerned with the perceptions that others have of a person; for example, how a woman is seen by her mother, her priest, and her lover.

A woman suffering from amnesia may forget who she is, and be unable to provide the police with her official name and address, but she would still report *that she is*, and so her sense of self would still be intact. Also, the perceptions that others have about her would differ, so that her mother would see her as one type of person and her husband would see her as another type, but such differences in perceived social selves would not change her basic sense of being. She would not feel her existence less or more as a result of her various social selves.

The Universal Sense of Self

The self, then, is a basic sense of being, as opposed to the markers of one's identity (personal identity), one's personal recollections and ideas about the self (self identity), or how others see one (social identity). Two characteristics are central to the self, and both of them are probably universal to all human societies.

First, the self must be singular. In all societies that we know about, persons who report that they are conscious of more than one being inside their body are considered abnormal, and most probably insane. Thus, the singular sense of self is an essentially normative feature of human experience. A second characteristic of the self is that it is experienced as continuous in time. For example, when a person wakes up in the morning, he senses that he is the same self who went to bed the previous night. He may begin the day by questioning his social identity ("How do others see me?") and under certain circumstances perhaps even his self identity ("I wonder what my real family name is?"), but a man with normal faculties would not begin the day by questioning if he is the same conscious being as he was some time ago ("Do I exist, or did that self die last night?").

The "Fleeting I"

Finally, we can demonstrate the unitary nature of the self, by reexamining the I/me distinction. It is a mistake to assume that the I and the me indicate the existence of different selves, because they are both simply terms that function to refer to the same entity: the singular self. This point becomes clear when we consider the problem sometimes referred to as "the fleeting I."

When we focus on the I, it immediately becomes the me. That is, it is impossible to focus on the I reporting on the me. This problem of the fleeting I suggests that, in fact, the I and the me are simply terms used to refer to the same single phenomenon: the sense of self.

If we use the Jamesian metaphor of the "stream of consciousness," we can conceptualize the self as being capable of changing places in this stream, so that it may move from one position to another. However, the self is only able to be in one place in the stream at any one time. Thus, just as a person cannot at the same time be conscious of an I and a me, a self cannot be in two places in the stream at the same time.

In the growing literature on the self, the vast majority of writers have discussed self-identity (the autobiographical information, evaluations, images, and the like that a person has) or social identity (how others see the person), rather than the self per se (a person's sense of conscious existence.

Having clarified the concept of self and distinguished it from self-identity and social identity, we are now in a better position to discuss related ideas, such as cultural differences in the self, self-actualization, and self-control.

Re-thinking the Self and Cultural Differences

Since the 1960s there has been a worldwide rising interest in ethnicity, associated with numerous separatist movements based on ethnic, linguistic, religious, and other criteria for category membership. In a climate where the celebration of diversity is a major theme in everyday life, it is perhaps inevitable that cultural diversity take center stage. In this context, culture is regarded not in the classic evaluative sense of "high" (e.g., classic music, opera, and so on) and low (e.g., pop music, soap operas, and the like), but in a nonevaluative sense that refers very broadly to everything influenced by humans, or more specifically to the way things are done here. The dramatic resurgence of culture as a topic of interest has led to a concern for cultural differences in just about every domain, including the self.

Research in traditional (e.g., India) and Western (e.g., U.S.) cultures has led some writers to claim that there are cultural differences in the self (Markus & Kitayama, 1991). Typically, Westerners are described as having selves that have very strong boundaries and are very mobile and independent from the group. People of traditional cultures, on the other hand, are described as having selves with much fuzzier boundaries, so that the distinction between the individual and the group is not as sharp.

A criticism raised against this point of view concerns individual responsibility. If the boundaries of selves are not sharply defined in some cultures, how can citizens be held responsible for any actions? For example, if an individual commits a murder, or wins a competition, or does anything else that in the West would merit punishment or reward, how can that person be held personally and uniquely responsible, if the self is seen to have vague boundaries and to be bound to the collectivity?

One way to respond to this criticism is to claim that whereas in individualistic societies responsibility is individual based, in collectivistic societies responsibility is much more group based. Thus, for example, in some tribal systems if a person from another tribe kills "one of us," then we hold the entire population of the other tribe responsible and attempt to kill any member of the other tribe, not necessarily the person who committed the murder. This kind of group-based responsibility and sense of justice would presumably be associated with a self with diffuse boundaries. Such an explanation, however, remains unsatisfactory even in the context of India and other traditional societies in the contemporary world, because they *do* have legal systems that work on the basis of individual responsibility. Individuals *are* held responsible for their actions in such societies.

But this leaves us with a puzzle: How can a self with diffuse boundaries be held responsible for any action? The solution to this dilemma is uncovered when we reexamine what "self" it is that is described by researchers as varying across cultures. It turns out to be personal identity and social identity, and *not* the self as a sense of conscious existence, that researchers refer to when they claim that the self varies across cultures.

Reexamining Self-Control

The dawn of the twenty-first century is not just the era of the self, but more specifically it is the era of people trying to exert self-control. From the covers of magazines, from television and radio commercials, from all kinds of media sources, we are told to take advantage of wonderful new programs designed to increase our self-control. To take control of ourselves seems to be the key to a happier life, to better health, to fulfillment in relationships and love life, to success at work, to just about everything we desire.

When we closely examine what is meant by self control in such discussions, we find that it is really the perceptions people have of themselves, the evaluative autobiographies that make up self-identity, that is the focus. A major concern of programs designed to help a person exert better self-control is to lead to a rethinking of self-identity, to see the self as one type of person rather than another. The assumption is that by changing perceptions of the self, it will be possible to change the self itself. The goal is really to change the way people think about themselves.

Examples of such programs are those designed to control weight, the "fat busters." These programs are now part of a huge and growing industry, involving a wide range of options, from direct drug therapy, such as pills that control appetite, to behavior therapy that uses support groups, reinforcement schedules, and the like. Weight control is a classic example of an area in which, in many cases, the "control" turns out to be illusory, with the result that people go through a yo-yo experience of gaining and losing weight, feeling bad and good about themselves, in cycles that seem to have no ending.

Most of the weight control programs that make up this multibillion dollar world industry lead to very little actual success. In the majority of cases, those in the programs gain back about 80 percent of the weight they lost within about a year, and all of it within five years. Set point theory proposes that the number of fat cells in the body becomes stabilized early in life, so weight control programs can only influence the size of the fat cells. Even though the size of fat cells can be decreased through dieting, there is a strong tendency for fat cells to return to a "set point," and hence for a person to return to a "set weight." This pessimistic scenario seems to be valid for the majority of people, although a minority seem to be able to loose weight as adults and maintain a lower weight level throughout their lives.

How, then, are we to explain the dramatic success of weight control programs, despite the hard evidence suggesting that in the majority of cases they do not enable people to lose weight over the long term? We believe the best explanation is based on illusions of control. These programs are financially successful because they are able to create for people the illusion that they have gained control of their own weight levels, even if control is in the short term.

Control of Internal and External Worlds

There is one area where the illusory nature of control in relation to the internal world of the self is particularly dangerous because it is designed to create an illusion related to the external world. This is the area of therapy, in particular methods such as attributional therapy (Abramson, 1988).

Attributional therapies are often designed to change self-identity, but they also create the illusion that the external world has changed. They work by altering the way people attribute causes to events. An attribution is a causal inference, a way of assigning a cause to an event. For example, a man takes a driving test and fails. He could attribute the cause of his failure to a variety of different factors and say: "I do not have enough driving experience"; "The examiner was a blind idiot!"; "The car I was driving had mechanical problems"; "It was a rainy day"; "My mother-in-law was in the car"; "I should have been wearing my glasses," and something similar.

Thousands of studies have shown that normal people have strong and systematic biases in the way they attribute causes to events. We generally make attributions in a way that makes us look good, at least to ourselves. If the outcome was bad, we see the cause as being external rather than internal to ourselves. Thus, the man in the preceding paragraph is more likely to see the "idiotic and blind examiner" as the cause of his failing the driving test than his own lack of driving ability. When something good happens, then we see the cause as being within ourselves. For example, in a good year a manager might say, "Why did my organization do so well this year? Obviously because I am a great manager." If, however, the results were not so good, the same manager might say, "Why did my organization do so poorly this year? Well, it has been a very difficult market."

One of my favorite ways to show such "self-serving" attributional biases is very risky because it works best when tried on couples living together, but after the experiment they may no longer stay together (Ross & Sicoly, 1979, this is one of the early studies on this bias). Ask each of the partners to independently estimate how much work he or she does around the house. You might phrase the question something like this: "Your place is always fairly tidy and there is food in the kitchen. Who does all of this work? What percentage of the cleaning up and shopping do you do personally?" The responses of typical couples appear on table 4.1.

Table 4.1
Estimated Division of the Workload

Type of Work	% of Work Done by Woman	Man	Total %
Cleaning	85	45	130
Shopping	75	50	125
Paperwork	60	80	140
Gardening	45	85	130
Serving Guests	90	45	135
Car Related	35	95	130

Having prepared such a table, you now face the dangerous task of bringing the couple together to try to explain to you (and each other!) why all of the percentages are well above 100. Who really is doing all the work anyway?

Such biased ways of making attributions seem to be"healthy," in so far as normal people are healthy. One of the key differences between normal people and individuals who experience severe depression is that the former tend to have strong self-serving biases in their attributions, whereas depressives tend not to have this particular bias (they actually may be more accurate in their attributions). A depressive is far more likely to say, "She would not marry me because I lack good looks and charisma." A "normal" person is more likely to conclude that "she would not marry me because she failed to see my real qualities" or that "she prefers the shallow personality types, like that superficially handsome and smart man she married." The fact of the matter is that depressives are going to be more truthful in such assessments, whereas normal people will make more biased attributions to make themselves look better.

In this topsy-turvy world, it should be no surprise that we have decided a smart way to make people less depressed is to get them to make less accurate and more self-serving attributions. Attributional therapy often involves training people to see the causes of events in such a way that they come out looking good and feeling good about themselves. It may well be that they had more accurate views about the world before, and that is why they got depressed (for example, one man actually recognized the fact that other people were not friendly toward him because they saw him as an empty-headed idiot!). By training people to see the world in a self-servingly biased manner, it is now possible to make them feel better.

Finally, attributional therapies ultimately work by changing our ideas about what controls events in the world. They represent a classic example of how perceptions of causal relations in the world, "what controls what," can be manipulated to become illusory. They also demonstrate the topsy-turvy nature of such situations, where to perceive illusory control is apparently more adaptive.

Concluding Comment

The adaptiveness of human behavior is, of course, dependent on cultural surroundings. Modern Western cultures glorify an independent and "self-controlled" view of the person. This creates a cultural context in which having self-control is prized. We prefer the illusion of self-control, and we are prepared to invest heavily to maintain this illusion. The multimillion dollar diet industry is just one indication of this trend.

Critical Thinking Exercises

(1) What is the self and why has self-control become such an important issue in industrialized societies?
(2) What are self-serving biases? Give examples from your everyday experiences.

5

Control and Rationality

Human beings often interpret their own actions *as if* they are in full control of the course of events. We are motivated to construct the world in a way that makes it appear that our plans have been implemented and have worked out the way we believed they would.

Consider, for example, an intriguing report of a plan to implement advanced high-tech warfare in an "electronic battlefield" training exercise. The exercise involved a mock battle between a conventional army and a high-tech army, and the plan was to demonstrate the superiority of the latter. However, The Washington Post (April 24, 1994) reported that events took a very different turn: "By the time a day of war games came to a close, the bad guys - the tank team without all the gee-whiz gizmos - had trounced their ultra-modern opposition." The newspaper report continued with this fascinating account:

> This [defeat] was inconvenient, since the Army had invited a large
> delegation of Pentagon Brass and reporters to its National Training
> Center for a demonstration of how advances in computerized digital
> communications will make U.S. tanks both more lethal to the enemy
> and less prone to killing their own soldiers with friendly fire.

Even more interesting for us is the reaction of the army planners to these unexpected turn of events: "Although a bit chagrined by the results on this particular day, Army leaders said they are not discouraged in their conviction that, once the bugs are worked out, digital technology will revolutionize the 21st century military machine."

In our everyday lives there are many instances where we maintain allegiances to our plans, even though actual events did not go according to plan. I was reminded of this recently by a friend who told me about his experience at a small train station in Switzerland. When his train arrived a few minutes late, the stationmaster climbed up a stepladder and put back the hands of the station clock so that the train would appear to be "on time" (it is a reflection of Swiss openness that this story was not censored by the Swiss co-author of this book).

Control Viewed from the Perspective of Rational and Irrational Models

Rational models of human behavior assume that humans are generally conscious of why they behave as they do and try to bring their thoughts and actions in line with one another. We are, according to rational models, always striving to be consistent beings, although we may sometimes distort or change our behavior in order to try to present ourselves as consistent. Cognitive psychology for the most part adopts a rational model of behavior.

Irrational models of behavior assume that humans are often unaware of the real reasons for the way they behave and are inconsistent in their thoughts and actions. No matter how hard we try to present ourselves as consistent and rational, we are in fact irrational beings. Psychodynamic psychology, particularly as represented by Sigmund Freud, adopts an irrationalist view.

Although they are different in some fundamental ways, rational and irrational models have illusions of control in common.

Control, Psychological Balance, and Rationality

In traditional Western psychology, the general assumption has been that people are motivated to maintain a state of psychological balance. We do this, supposedly, by altering our ideas or our actions so that they are in harmony with one another. This process can be unconscious, but it inevitably involves some level of control by us of our thoughts and actions. We have already discussed self-serving biases in chapter 4, but the issue of psychological balance and control is broader.

For example, I ran across a friend I had not seen for several years and discovered that she had married David, one of two young men who were her suitors the last time we met. At that time, she had said that she was not really interested in David and that Richard, the second suitor, was by far her favorite. She and Richard made detailed plans for their wedding, their honeymoon, their new home, and even the number of children they would have. Richard, who worked for an international corporation, was promoted to a new post abroad, and the wedding plans fell apart after he moved. I remember this painful incident very well because it caused my friend considerable grief and many sleepless nights. Now, however, she told me that everything had worked out just as she had planned, that she never really intended to marry Richard, and that she and David were always meant for each other. This behavior is self-serving, but more importantly it allows (at least the illusion of) balance to be maintained.

Psychological Balance and Rational Beings

An important assumption in Western models of human behavior is that, for the most part, people are rational. The cognitive revolution gained momentum in the 1950s and 1960s, at a time when computers were becoming more powerful and more readily available to researchers and the general public. The model of humans as computers took hold of the imagination of researchers and laypeople alike. Just as computers have hardware and software, humans have hardware (physiological characteristics) and software (mental processes). Both humans and computers communicate through language (see Fiske & Taylor, 1991, for a review of research adopting this approach).

The model of humans as thinking machines idealizes rational thinking. Problem solving becomes a matter of efficiency, using the most direct and least expensive routes. The focus is on the performance capabilities of the machine, isolated from the environment.

Reality caught up with researchers in the 1980s, when the limits of the thinking machine model began to show themselves. Human thinking is often influenced by emotions. Thoughts are often effected by anger, shame, sadness, and many other such experiences (see Parrott, 1993). Of course, computers might be programmed to mimic shame or anger, but such science fiction possibilities have so far not been realized effectively.

We know that a human being can make a wrong decision because of anger, but what would it mean if a computer made a wrong decision for this reason? A computer may mimic anger, but the *social* meaning of a computer "deciding out of anger" would be different. Here is an important dividing line between human behavior and computer behavior. It is not necessarily that they differ in terms of what happens inside the mind of the person and that of the computer, but that they differ in terms of the social meaning of their behavior (Harré, 1994).

Related to this distinction is another major limitation of the rational model; humans are influenced by ideology and ideals. They have biased views about the kind of distribution of resources that should take place in society. They often twist and turn their arguments so as to support certain decisions and negate other ones. The head of R&D may well give a biased report on a favorite research project in order to get more funding for it next year, even if it means giving a report that is biased against other projects with as much or even more promise.

In just about every domain of human life, it is irrationality rather than rationality that most often prevails. Anyone in doubt of this should spend some time working at a university, where people are supposed to be educated in rational thinking. Ironically, professors and experts trained to think rationally often act on the basis of irrational fears, likes, and dislikes. Anyone who has been in the midst of a battle, or even just a skirmish, in academic politics will attest to its being particularly destructive, vindictive, and irrational.

However, if one interrupts academics in the midst of a bloody battle, they would do their best to justify their behavior as rational.

Irrationality and Control

Although academic psychology has been dominated by rational models of human behavior, clinical psychology and other applied therapy domains have a strong tendency to depict humans as irrational. This is famously represented by the work of Sigmund Freud. Illusions of control also play an essential role in Freud's model, and society is seen as playing a conspiratorial role. Personality development begins with the id (blind strivings for immediate gratification of needs), at which stage the infant is egocentric and moved by the pleasure principle, the urge to satisfy desires instantly with no concern for the consequences such pleasure seeking has on others. Through interactions with others, there gradually develops within the infant a sense of societal norms and rules. The constraints of the real world impose themselves. Gradually, the normative system of society is internalized, so there now exists an ego (reactions that attempt to reconcile the immediate satisfaction demanded by the id with the limitations of the real world) and superego (the internalized value system of society) alongside the id. A "conscience" has grown, like an alien being whose seed is planted by society and nurtured through constant reinforcement by parents, teachers, and other agents of socialization.

Freud teaches us that during the process of socialization, there occurs a repression of thoughts and desires that are forbidden by the norms of society. Foremost among these are various sexual desires, sex being an area in which social taboos are particularly strict. Repressed desires are submerged into the unconscious, but reveal themselves through a variety of channels, such as dreams, slips of the tongue, and "accidents." At the level of the conscious, however, individuals experience illusions of control, imagining that they are actually and consciously in control of their own thoughts of actions.

Concluding Comment

Human beings are motivated to see themselves as rational, and social scientists have obliged by providing models of behavior that depict people as rational. The model of humans as thinking machines reflects this trend. Actual human behavior, however, shows that we often behave irrationally. We sometimes do not know why we do things, and what we do can have terrible consequences (as in the case of actions leading to war, for example). However, we are excellent at rationalizing our own behavior after the fact. In looking back to explain the past, even world wars are rationalized.

Critical Thinking Exercises

(1) What is meant by rational behavior and the model of humans as thinking machines?

(2) Give examples of irrational and rational behavior from your everyday life.

6

Conspiracies and Tokens: The Psycho-Political Picture of Control

The newspaper headlines in the United States were almost all about the campaign finance report that day back in 1997 when we authors of this book were scheduled to meet at the main railway station in Washington, D.C. One of us was arriving by train from New York, and we had a week of intense research and writing ahead of us. The other waited for the train to arrive, browsing around a magazine stand.

> A man looking at the newspaper headlines said in a disgusted voice:
> "They are all in it together, damned politicians. They're in the pockets of the rich. I don't trust the government, any government."
> "Maybe if you bothered to vote you could get somebody you like in office." This comment came from his female companion.
> "What's the use," he snapped back, "It's all made up by them."

They walked away, leaving listeners to wonder exactly how elections are "made up" by "them." This brief episode serves to highlight the role of conspiracies in the larger society. Some people strongly believe in conspiracies by unknown others to control political and economic life, and they act or refuse to act (as in the case of a person refusing to vote) on this basis.

The Centrality of Conspiracy

Modern thinkers from a wide range of backgrounds have proposed, often explicitly, that it is functional in one way or another not only for people to have actual control but also for them to *believe* they have control of events inside and/or outside themselves. Among such thinkers are political theorists such as Karl Marx (1818-1883) and Vilfredo Pareto (1848-1923), humanistic therapists such as Carl

Rogers and Abraham Maslow, as well as more empirically oriented experimental researchers such as Martin Seligman. At the head of any such list, inevitably, comes the controversial founder of psychoanalysis, Sigmund Freud (1856-1939).

Of course, by the 1990s it had become the norm to regard Marx and Freud as belonging to "the junkyard of history," and to declare that they are no longer of any significance. Such a perspective is fundamentally misguided because, in a sense, we are all Marxists and Freudians now. Some of the ideas, concepts, and terminology of Marxism (e.g., "religion is the opium of the people," "class conflict," "capitalist/proletariate") and Freudian psychoanalysis ("Freudian slip," "displacement," "suppression," "unconscious") have so pervaded our everyday language and thinking that it is not an exaggeration to state that they have become embedded in, and inseparable from, modern culture. Although Marxism and Freudian psychoanalysis have not withstood the test of time as intact models, many of their ideas have thrived separately and become an integral part of modern culture in industrialized and also in many developing countries.

A central theme in the systems of Marx and Freud is the concern with "conspiracies to control." As we shall see, a number of other writers, particularly the Italian Niccolo Machiavelli (1469-1527), also make uniquely original contributions to this theme.

The Conspiratorial Mind

Machiavelli's writings, particularly as exemplified in *The Prince*, act as an important point of origin for modern conspiratorial models. Like the later conspiracy theorists (particularly Marx, Pareto, and Freud) Machiavelli found himself in deep trouble with various authorities, especially the Catholic church (Machiavelli, 1640/1961). For a long time, his writings were banned in various Western countries, and he was denounced from pulpits as a personification of the devil. What exactly had he done to deserve this fate?

Machiavelli was what, in modern terms, we would refer to as a career diplomat, and he wrote *The Prince* after the *Medici* came back to power and "offered" him early retirement (as well as a brief spell in jail). In assessing *The Prince*, we should keep in mind the picture of Machiavelli in forced retreat at his estate near San Casciano, devoting himself to a work that would show how he could again be useful to the rulers of the day.

Machiavelli, perhaps writing tongue-in-cheek, provided advice to rulers about how to retain control and extend their hold over a population. The advice was designed to be effective, but seemed to suggest that power is retained by rulers without much concern for moral issues. The explicit goal in Machiavelli's formula was the retention and extension of power, and any concern for ethics and moral values seemed only to arise indirectly.

Of course, if rulers needed to be seen as moral and ethical in order to retain power, then they could present themselves as moral and ethical. However,

Machiavelli's writings implied that in practice moral and ethical values do not prevent rulers from doing whatever it takes to retain power.

Illusions of control become useful because rulers could fool the ruled into thinking that they have some control over events. The multitudes need not know what is really going on behind the scenes, but those of them who have to be included in power politics and do know could be persuaded that they have some level of control.

A benign explanation for why Machiavelli received such condemnation from the ecclesiastic critics, some of whom seemed to wish Machiavelli could be resurrected only so that they could crucify him properly, is that he was giving princes and other leaders "un-Godly" advice and in general acting as a corrupting influence. An alternative explanation is that Machiavelli had actually put his finger on how rulers, including princes of the Church, went about their business of gaining and retaining power and control over people. In short, this alternative interpretation suggests that those in power found him dangerous because he was a "whistle blower."

The condemnation of authorities seemed only to spread Machiavelli's fame ever wider over the next few centuries. His ideas have even influenced modern empirical social science research in the United States, as reflected by measures of a "Machiavellian personality trait." Initiated by Richard Christie and Florence Geise, this research began in the 1960s and helped to identify behavioral characteristics of individuals who score high on Machiavellianism, characterized by a tendency to see the world as a threatening place, to see a need to cut corners, deceive others, and believe that "nice guys finish last." The latter of these is particularly damaging for authorities because if nice guys finish last, then those in power positions must be the not-so-nice guys.

Conspiracies and Social Classes

Although Machiavelli was vehemently denounced and drummed out of the Church, the hostility directed at him was rather diffuse, and in many cases it was sporadic. This may be because Machiavelli's ideas did not amount to a formal ideology that could be used as a basis for political organizations. Thus, he was ultimately condemned as an individual source of corruption, rather than a source of organized political movements or parties that hoped to seize power.

Two conspiratorial thinkers of the "grand" tradition emerged in the middle of the nineteenth and the turn of the twentieth centuries. Their writings formed the basis of formal ideological movements and effective political organizations. They were Marx and Pareto, two thinkers who marched alongside each other for so much of the conceptual road, only to dramatically change direction at a critical stage in their models of group relationships. Marx's ideas acted as the framework for numerous political organizations and governments, the largest being the former USSR, while Pareto's ideas influenced fascist regimes, particularly in the early part

of the twentieth century in Italy and elsewhere. As we shall see, however, more recent adaptations of Pareto's theory have been described as being compatible with democracy and meritocracy (Dye & Zeigler, 1970).

The conspiracy of the rulers against the ruled becomes even more elaborate in the writings of Marx and Pareto than in those of Machiavelli, and the role of illusions of control is even more prominent and explicit. There are remarkable similarities in the basic tenets of the first part of the models developed by these two thinkers. Both Marx and Pareto believed that societies everywhere are ruled by an elite, and they saw governments merely as "fronts," part of a smoke screen to serve the interests of such ruling groups (Marx, 1852/1979; Pareto, 1935). From this perspective, labels such as "democracy" and "liberalism" (and, for Pareto, even "communism") are all smokescreens, designed to fool the nonelite into thinking that they have some control over the way society is governed. (Pareto would probably have had an "I told you so" attitude if he had been a witness when the full corruption of the Eastern bloc countries was exposed, and the inequalities existing in supposedly communist societies such as Czechoslovakia became public knowledge.)

From this perspective, then, the elite are motivated to control in actuality, but they are also motivated to create illusions of control for the masses, to lead the masses to believe they are participating in government. However, Marx explicitly went beyond this. In his view it is also essential that the elite come to believe in the illusions they have themselves created. It is through the acceptance of their own illusions, according to Marx, that the elite are able to maintain faith in social systems that are actually unjust. Like modern psychologists of the "equity" tradition, Marx recognized the need people have to see the world as just and fair.

Perhaps the most fundamental difference between Marx and Pareto is that the former saw societies as evolving in a stage-wise manner toward an inevitable endstate, whereas the latter assumed the historical development of societies was cyclical. Marx believed that, just as capitalism followed feudalism, socialism inevitably follows capitalism. The capitalist system will inevitably collapse because the competing economic interests of capitalists and the proletariate, those who own the means of production and those who must sell their labor on the marketplace, will lead them to repeatedly clash during ever-more intense and destructive cycles of economic growth and depression, booms and busts. Through these clashes, the proletariate will gradually recognize that their class has economic interests that compete with those of the capitalist class. The emergence of such class consciousness will lead to even sharper class conflict, with the end result being revolution and a takeover of power by the proletariate.

For some time following the proletariate revolution, society will be ruled through a dictatorship of the proletariate. Gradually, a classless society will evolve and a new form of collective consciousness will emerge among the population, one in which the rights of the collectivity will be seen by everyone as having priority over the rights of individuals. People will work to benefit society, rather than themselves personally. The end result of this inevitable process will be a classless society, one in which government and other forms of central control disappear. People will develop the consciousness to make their contributions to society without central supervision.

Marx and Pareto were generally in agreement about the role of central governments, which they saw as acting to protect the interests of the "real" rulers (in Pareto's terms the elite, in Marx's terms the capitalists) who often use politicians as a front. Marx believed that societies move from stage to stage and arrive at an ideal endpoint; but Pareto dismissed such ideas as unrealistic and argued that all societies throughout history have been, and will continue to be, ruled by elites.

Pareto's definition of the elite was based on talent. Among every group of people, some are more talented than others, and this talent allows them to gain power and exert control over the group. The elite who rule a society can only remain in power by keeping their group open, so that talented outsiders can move up to join them, and those born to elite parents but lacking high talent can move down to join the nonelite. Pareto believed that this "circulation of the elite" is essential for any system to survive, in this he followed an example set twenty-four hundred years earlier by Plato in *The Republic*.

Pareto pointed out that the elite generally cause their own downfall by closing ranks and not allowing circulation. He described history as the "graveyard of the aristocracy" because each aristocratic group digs its own grave by preventing circulation. When the elite prevent movement up and down the social hierarchy, there is an accumulation of talented persons who form a potential counter-elite among the nonelite, and a buildup of nontalented people among the elite. The end result is that the counter-elite mobilize the masses to revolt and overthrow the elite, who are paralyzed by the accumulation of nontalented people in their own ranks.

Once the counter-elite lead the nonelite to victory, they display their true colors by establishing themselves as the new elite and by brushing aside their former promises to reform the system (one cannot help but be reminded of contemporary politicians). They maintain the hierarchical structure of society, with its inequalities of power and resource distribution, and only make cosmetic changes. In essence, the counter-elite become the new elite and enjoy all of the privileges of the former elite. The new elite continue to use the government apparatus to control the nonelite, and thus to perpetuate the conspiracy.

This cyclical, and some would say "cynical," view of society has not carried favor with many modern thinkers. However, a more optimistic version of elite theory was offered by Gaetano Mosca, another Italian researcher, and this version influenced some late twentieth-century writers to argue that elite theory is compatible with democracy. Two concepts are critical here: accountability and circulation. First, although democratic societies are ruled by the elite, they are accountable to the nonelite and can be voted out of office. Second, democratic societies are meritocratic, and thus they allow the circulation of the elite that Pareto saw as being essential to the survival of all systems. The end of meritocracy would mean the end of circulation and, thus, the collapse of a system (through the accumulation of talented people in the nonelite, the formation of the counter-elite, a revolution lead by the counter-elite, and all the other steps in the process described by Pareto).

Self-Determination

Marx's theory is often described as being an economic model of historical change because of the primacy it gives to economic factors. For Marx, social relations and individual consciousness follow economic relations and the position of people in the production process. The role he conceived for psychological factors, although important, was a dependent one. For example, class consciousness was a prerequisite for class mobilization and revolution; thus, in a sense, psychological factors had to be in place for a revolution to begin. However, class consciousness could only come about (the negation of "false consciousness") if the economic situation led to open conflicts between capitalists and the proletariate. Without such actual conflict, the proletariate would not become conscious of their real interests.

Consequently, in Marx's system conscious self-determination plays a role within the limits set by economic processes. When the proletariate revolution comes about, the economic conditions are created that will lead to a consciousness that allows a classless society to emerge. In turn, this new classless consciousness creates a situation whereby the central government naturally disappears. If one was to ask what the primary source for changes leading to this classless society was, Marx would be respond that it was economic changes.

To create the necessary material conditions for a classless society to evolve, Marxist regimes created strong and highly centralized governments, such as occurred in the former USSR. A central characteristic of such governments was the long-term, centralized planning they undertook. It is now a matter of historical record that such planning did not work effectively. The prediction and control achieved by such central governments was illusory, and the huge systems built on these illusions inevitably collapsed.

In sharp contrast to this Marxist system where primacy is given to economic conditions, we find the American dream, the topic of the next chapter, an ideal of individual persons determining their own destinies and "beating the economic odds" to move in new directions.

Concluding Comment

The illusion that "I am in control" is sometimes overshadowed by suspicions, even deep convictions, that "they are in control." The idea that society can be controlled by unseen hands, a powerful elite hidden behind an ideological smoke screen, is central to Machiavelli, Marx, Pareto, and other conspiratorial writers. In practice, the world has proven to be too complex and unwieldy to be controlled by any hands, seen or unseen.

Critical Thinking Exercises

(1) Instead of seeing themselves in control, people with conspiratorial minds see others in control. Explain and give examples.

(2) What is the difference between the controls that Pareto and Marx see in society?

7

The American Dream:
A Basis for a Grand Illusion
of Control

But they were young and healthy, and they worked hard, very hard. My father said that for two years he washed dishes somewhere in the basement of a big hotel and he never saw the sun. He would start work before the sun came up and go home after it went down, seven days a week. They saved money, opened their own restaurant. They put me and my sister through college, and now our children are really benefiting. My son is a millionaire at thirty-seven! That's success, that's the American dream!

Retired manager.

The story of the American dream is so well known, yet still so fresh. It is so often told, yet never tiring. We all enjoy hearing about success, and the glamour of success in the American dream never seems to fade. It is a rainbow that is always present, waiting to inspire us when we feel gloomy. Yet, hard statistics tell us that this dream is not any more, or any less, true in America than it is in other societies. The mobility of individuals up the social hierarchy is not any more, or any less, likely to occur in the United States than it is in other Western societies. Even the American middle class has "fallen from grace" and experienced a decrease in real earnings since the late 1970s (see Newman, 1988). It is a mistake to seek the secret to the dream's appeal by looking at hard facts. The American dream is attractive for the same reason that Marx's dream appeals. It presents us with a glimpse of paradise and makes us feel we can control events so that we can end up in paradise.

The American dream has even more appeal than Marxism because it affects us at a much more personal level. It is about individual human stories, something tangible and at hand, rather than the abstract "economic forces" Marx talks about. In Marx's vision of the world, the ultimate fate of people is determined first and

foremost by larger material conditions and economic processes, factors outside of the person. In the American dream, characteristics of the single individual and psychological processes, factors inside the person, determine outcome. These two competing pictures stand at opposite poles, although in practice they share a vital characteristic in that neither are realized in their pure forms.

In Letters from an American Farmer, first published in 1782, Crevecoeur (1735-1813) provided what is perhaps the most inspired and eloquent description of how some people have idealized the New World and the American dream (Crevecoeur, 1782/1985). Addressing the question, What is an American? Crevecoeur answered by saying that Americans are people who leave behind them all "ancient" prejudices of class, religion, and so on, to enter into a New World, where "individuals of all nations are melted into a new race whose labors and prosperity will one day cause great changes in the world" (p. 396).

An Open New World

Most important, an American should love America more than the land of her or his origin because "here the rewards of his industry follow with equal steps the progress of his labor" (Crevecoeur, 1782/1985, p.396). In many other passages in his writings Crevecoeur elaborated on this same idea, the American belief that the rewards received by people depend on personal talent and hard work. Because society is open and free of all prejudices, individuals move up and down the social hierarchy depending on how talented they are and how hard they work. Thus, self-help and individual responsibility become the slogans for the New World. This sets the stage for the growth of a strong belief in personal control over personal destiny. The American dream, that anyone can make it in America if only they have talent and work hard, is played out hundreds of times each day in the modern media, the stories children read in their classes, and many other ways.

Rags to Riches, One More Time

The most powerful personification of the American dream is the self-made person from an immigrant family, bringing to life the image of rags to riches. Such personalities are admired in most parts of the world, but it is in America that they are idolized. This is how Lee Iacocca, now an American legend, began his rags-to-riches autobiography and the start of his immigrant life in the United States:

> Nicola Iacocca, my father, arrived in this country in 1902 at the age of twelve - poor, alone, and scared . . . . As the boat sailed into New York Harbor, my father looked out and saw the Statue of Liberty, that great symbol of hope for millions of immigrants. . . For Nicola. . . America was the land of freedom - the freedom to become anything you wanted to be, if you wanted it badly enough and were willing to work for it. (Iacocca, 1984, p.3).

Iacocca went on to explain that his father, "was in love with America, and he pursued the American dream with all his might" (1984, p.5).

The power of the American dream reflects how strongly Americans want to believe they have control over their personal destinies. Even though in practice there is a very low probability that an individual will achieve the rags-to-riches rise so often publicized in the media, the belief in such a possibility persists. This optimism is intimately associated with the American dream, because in America, as Scarlett says in Margaret Mitchell's uniquely American tale, *Gone with the Wind*, "Tomorrow is another day."

The Power of Tokenism

There is a sharp contrast between the reality of individual mobility in the social hierarchy of the United States and the "fairy tale" of extensive upward mobility as depicted by the American dream. For certain, *some* individuals do realize the rags-to-riches mobility idealized in "the dream," but the hard evidence clearly shows that their numbers are very limited. Given this situation, how is the dream kept alive? How is the illusion maintained that individuals control their own destinies and can move up in the social hierarchy? A key to this is tokenism.

As long as a small number of individuals move up the social system, then people perceive the system as open. Even if the number of individuals who make it to the top is very small, these "tokens" will be effective in making the system appear open. The available evidence shows that people, at least in Western cultures, tend to say, "If there is a chance that somebody can get to the top, if there is an opening, then why not me? And if I don't make it, why not my children?"

Concluding Comment

The enormous appeal of the American dream is in its promise of control. The American dream gives individuals hope that they control their own destinies. It is an ideology that allows the downtrodden, the poor, the powerless, the homeless (and even the middle-class manager) to say: "I can do it, the road is open and all I have to do is move fast enough and far enough ahead. There is no telling what I can do, if I only try!"

Critical Thinking Exercises

(1) The power of the American dream rests on the assumption that society is open. That is why the law had to be changed to give African Americans and other minorities equal rights. Explain this statement.

(2) Does the American dream endorse the view that control is internal or external to the person?

8

Controlling our Childrens' Future: Or Why the Next Generation Seems so Obstinate to Go Its own Way

"He's at that stage now," explained the mother. "He throws tantrums every single day. They all do that, the terrible twos."

She was pointing to a small, wiry little boy, busy amusing himself by spraying his mother's perfume on their cat.

"I had better not take it away from him, or he'll throw another tantrum. He's at that stage you know."

The cat, irritated but finely perfumed, managed to escape through an open window.

It is not just parents of "terrible twos" who assume that human behavior moves according to predictable stages. The most influential psychological models of human development, such as those espoused by the Swiss psychologist Jean Piaget and the American Lawrence Kohlberg, are what is best described as stage models (see Flavell, 1963; Inhelder & Piaget, 1958, 1964; Kohlberg, 1984). That is, they assume that human development takes place in a sequential, stage-wise manner, with all humans predictably moving from one stage to the next, according to a predetermined timetable.

Developmental Stages and Control

The idea of predetermination is at the heart of the issue here. The assumption that human development moves in a predetermined stage-wise manner implies that at any given time psychologists can predict what the next event will be, how the child will "grow" next, in which direction she or he will move ahead, and in what areas she or he will not change. Thus, development is seen to be predictable and "under the control" of invisible stages. Our main argument in this chapter is that the entire stage or "sequential" approach to human development is misguided.

The stages identified by psychologists such as Piaget, Kohlberg, and Maslow are themselves social constructions. This underlines the importance we give to culture as an influence on human behavior. At the same time, however, this does not imply that culture can control individuals because people enjoy some measure of free will in deciding which norms and rules they will follow, and which ones they will reject. For example, one of us (the authors) is extremely well attired and follows the norms and rules appropriate for a well-dressed gentleman, while the other follows other norms and rules. Neither is forced to dress one way or the other. After pointing out major shortcomings in the stage models in the first part of this chapter, we follow with, we present an alternative "thematic" view of development in the second part.

Reassessing Stage Models of Development

Most humans are able to crawl by their eighth month, and walk by their fourteenth month, but they are unable to run before they begin to crawl and walk, just as they cannot speak in sentences before they are able to use single words. Such widely observed and recognized "sequential" behavior change seems to intuitively lead us to build "stage models" of development and to use a "staircase" metaphor to describe human development. Despite their intuitive appeal, however, stage models of development suffer from a number of shortcomings (see figure 8.1), three of which are discussed below (for a related discussion, see Field, 1981).

First, stage models typically underestimate the abilities of children. For example, Piaget claimed that children younger than six or seven are not yet able to use the operations of reversibility and compensation. Consequently, they cannot conserve. In a typical conservation study, children are shown two identical beakers filled to the same level with water, and the content of one beaker is poured into a different shaped beaker so that the two columns of water are now of unequal height. The ability to make conservation judgments is attained if the child recognizes that each beaker has the same amount of water. Contrary to Piaget's propositions, research suggests that children as young as four years can be trained to conserve. Similarly, there is evidence that in some situations children as young as three years old are not egocentric. This is at a much earlier age than predicted by Piaget. Kohlberg's accounts also underestimate what children are capable of doing. For example, children as young as about seven years of age have been found to use moral reasoning at the "highest" of Kohlberg's stages.

One reason for the underestimation of abilities among the young may be the use of the laboratory as the context for conducting studies. For example, studies of word learning in naturalistic settings show that children acquire new words very rapidly. In contrast, laboratory studies show word learning to be painfully slow.

Second, stage models underestimate the influence of training on behavior (Cole & Cole, 1993). This is associated with a tendency to confuse culture and biology as sources of the stages identified by researchers. For example, many of the characteristics of stages described by Piaget as being biologically determined can be fundamentally influenced by training. Similarly, Kohlberg's model confuses biological sources of stages with cultural sources. His proposition that moral reasoning proceeds along three broad stages, preconventional, conventional, and postconventional, or principled, reasoning, is challenged by evidence suggesting that the same individual, whether a child or an adult, can use moral reasoning at each of these three levels, depending on circumstances (Elmer & Hogan, 1981).

In one study using adult subjects, individuals were found to change their attitudes toward fundamental human rights, such as free speech, depending on the particular country in which a violation took place and their own levels of conservativism and religiosity (Moghaddam & Vuksanovic, 1990). In another study, respondents of right, left, and moderate political orientations completed a moral-reasoning task from their own perspective and then from the perspectives of an extreme conservative and an extreme radical (Elmer, 1983). The results revealed that right-wing and moderate respondents showed significant increases in their principled reasoning scores when they adopted the perspective of the radical. These findings support the argument that most adults are capable of using moral reasoning at all the levels identified by Kohlberg, but they choose to argue at particular level(s), depending on circumstances.

A third shortcoming of stage models is their description of human development in terms of discrete stages, rather than as a series of continuous, flexible themes. In Piaget's account people pass through discrete stages in a step-wise and unidirectional manner, with passage from each stage being a condition for transition to the next stage. Similarly, in Kohlberg's model, people who make moral decisions at the conventional level do not also make such decisions at the preconventional and principled levels. Likewise, Maslow's (1970) need-hierarchy model assumes a step-wise progression, involving five levels of needs: physiological, safety, love, status, self-actualization. Each need is assumed to be "activated" only when the preceding level of need has been satisfied. For example, love needs are assumed to be activated only when safety needs are satisfied, and safety needs are activated only when physiological needs are satisfied.

Contrary to Maslow's account, however, available evidence, such as Alderfer's (1972) "existence, relatedness, and growth" ("ERG") model, supports an explanation that depicts needs as continuous. Alderfer's existence needs correspond to Maslow's physiological and safety needs, his relatedness needs correspond to Maslow's love needs, and his growth needs correspond to Maslow's esteem and self-actualization needs. The most important difference is that in Alderfer's model all the needs can simultaneously be incorporated in behavior. For example, a person may be influenced by existence, relatedness, and growth needs at the same time.

Thus, empirical research suggests that the different types of cognitive abilities described by Piaget, the various moral decision-making approaches outlined by

Kohlberg, and the different needs incorporated in Maslow's model are best conceived as continuous themes. This is becoming apparent as evidence pertaining to the stage models accumulates. This is not to imply that all skills are acquired at the same age by a person. Obviously, the attainment of some skills requires greater training than others. Rather, it proposes that (1) the acquisition of basic skills is continuous and very often simultaneous and (2) people can acquire a set of skills without being "stuck" at a stage. This means that people can use skills A, B, and C when they want to, but shift to E, F and G when it better suits them.

On the one hand the influential stage models have often underestimated the abilities of children, and on the other hand these models have tended to confuse biological and cultural sources of stages. In addition, these models have assumed discrete stages where they should have considered continuous and simultaneously active themes in behavior. Although the influence of biological factors is evident at the very early stages of development, once this initial period is over, the behavior of individuals is "engulfed" by culture. For example, children as young as seven years of age are soon able to reason at all the different stages described by Kohlberg, but they choose to reason at a particular level depending on circumstances. Longitudinal studies involving Kohlberg himself show similar variability in moral development (Colby, Kohlberg, Gibbs, & Lieberman, 1983).

Some of the confusion in this area can be cleared up by further clarifying the meaning of the term "universal" and by focusing on culture as a source of developmental stages.

Do "Universals" Signify Biological Determinacy?

One of the avowed goals of psychology, including cross-cultural adaptations of the discipline, is to identify "universals" of behavior. The general assumption has been that the way to discover universals is to examine behavior in many different cultures and identify similarities. For example, if preconventional thinking is characteristic of moral thinking among children at a certain age in a several cultures, and no culture has been found to differ from this pattern, then this behavior must represent a universal. A fatal error is made, however, when such "universals" are assumed to arise from biological factors, and hence are accounted for by "genetic epistemology."

In summary, then, stage models have portrayed human development in ways that are too rigid, and also in some instances assumed the source of behavior to be genetic, when the source is just as likely, or even more likely, to be cultural. Although some critics of stage models may have misdirected their attacks (e.g., Macnamara & Austin, 1993; Siegel, 1993), there seems to be general consensus that greater emphasis on continuity and on themes in development is particularly appropriate. But what would an alternative "thematic" account of human development be like? Let us turn to this question next, using person-group relations, an important aspect of social development, as the specific focus for consideration.

Thematic Rather than "Staircase" Development

By drawing up a thematic picture of human social development and moving away from the "staircase" metaphor, we are in agreement with a number of scholars in child development research. Specifically, Siegler has recently introduced an "overlapping wave" metaphor for cognitive development, proposing that individuals may use many different ways of thinking about the world at any time in their development (Siegler, 1995). Siegler reported data showing that young children use different ways of thinking about numbers, including length (if the length of the row of coins is the same, then the number must be the same), but the same individuals who use length sometimes also use counting or switch to some other strategy (such as saying, "I don't know"), depending on what has worked before and the feedback they have received.

Both biological and cultural influences remain important in person-group relations throughout the lives of individuals. However, we can identify an earlier period during which the total dependency of infants on others for their survival makes biological needs the basis of relationships. During a second period, although biological influences continue to play a part, it is culture that has the major influence. Instead of conceiving of stages in development, this model assumes there are a variety of themes. Although several themes can be present simultaneously, some themes are more prominent than others at any one period in a person's life. We might envisage this as a symphony concert, with the strings, wind instruments, percussion instruments, and so on each bringing to life different themes.

Implications for Control

We have argued that human social and psychological development does not take place within the framework of sequential stages. The implication, made explicit in our account, is that there is a great deal more plasticity in human development than the models of Piaget, Kohlberg, Maslow, and other stage-theorists would have us believe. We must, however, return to the mystery of why such stage models, with their obvious weaknesses, continue to enjoy such strong support in traditional social sciences. For example, the models of Piaget and Kohlberg continue to be tremendously influential in the domain of education, and that of Maslow has a place in just about every discussion about motivation, management, and work. How are we to explain this mystery?

It seems to us that the best explanation is the strong motivation pervasive among modern social scientists to see events, and human behavior particularly, as controllable. This is reflected in the adoption of causal models of behavior in the social sciences, including traditional psychology, sociology, and economics. The stage conception of human development is causal in the sense that it assumes human behavior is causally determined, in this case by the built-in stages of development.

In response to the question, "why did the girl behave in this way?" a stage-model explanation would have us believe that her behavior is caused by her stage of cognitive, social, moral, or other kinds of development. This implies that she could not do otherwise, even if she intended to, because she is trapped within a particular developmental stage. There is little room, then, for human agency in these stage models. More relevant to the theme of our book, such models try to maintain the illusion that human behavior is predictable and under control.

Concluding Comment

The stage models of human development seem reassuring from one perspective. They give us the impression that we can understand, predict, and even control human behavior. For example, if a little boy is spraying the cat with mom's perfume, it is because he is at the terrible-two stage, and there are experts to tell us how to control terrible twos. Such stages are only social constructions. The terrible-two stage plagues American families, but is absent from Japan and other eastern cultures. The same thing is true of the so-called middle-age crisis that has hit many Americans during the late tentieth century. Such experiences arise out of cultural rather than biological sources and are local rather than universal.

Critical Thinking Exercises

(1) Stage models give the impression that human development is predictable and controllable. Describe examples of such models.
(2) Stage models are appealing because they simplify life for us. We can say that Joe is at stage X so that is why he behaves in this way. Give illustrative examples from your everyday life.

9

Control and the Unofficial Organization: A Story of Neglect

Alice sighed wearily, I think you might do something better with the time, she said, than waste it in asking riddles that have no answers.

'If you knew Time as well as I do,' said the Hatter, 'you wouldn't talk about wasting *it*. It's *him*.'

'I don't know what you mean,' said Alice.

'Of course you don't!' the Hatter said, tossing his head contemptuously. 'I dare say you never even spoke to Time!'

'Perhaps not,' Alice cautiously replied: 'but I know I have to beat time when I learn music.'

'Ah! that accounts for it,' said the Hatter. 'He won't stand beating. Now, if you only kept on good terms with him, he'd do almost anything you liked with the clock.

Alice's Adventures in Wonderland (Lewis Carroll)

Looking at an organizational chart or a formal job description, reading a strategic plan, listening to a mission statement, such activities can make us feel that we are sharing experiences much as Alice did. If we are employees of a complex organization, then organizational charts and other facets of the formal seem rather "unreal."

Anyone who has ever worked in complex organizations can point to numerous instances when the informal way of doing things is followed, and accepted as the best way (although the informal organization remains neglected in research, texts that use a case study approach inevitably highlight the importance of the informal organization; for example, see Wagner & Hollenback, 1992). For instance, new employees are routinely hired and promoted through procedures that deviate from the official company guidelines, without the charge being made that such hiring and promotion is a "mistake" *because* the guidelines were not followed. In every corporation there can be found cases of employees who were hired without having the degree qualifications required for their positions, but who nevertheless proved to be extremely successful in their work.

Moreover, after being hired employees are supposed to be promoted according to formal career-planning systems, but key managerial promotions are often made on the basis of the human chemistry between top executives and individual managers.

A close scrutiny of employee interactions in major corporations shows there are many differences between the official way to work and how business is actually conducted. Such differences between the official and actual ways of doing business do not mean that employees are accused of being mistaken.

The Functions of the "Formal Organization"

The formal organization, as depicted in organizational charts and job descriptions, is only one construction or version of the organization. This official version only exists in legal documents. This is not to deny the fundamental influence of the formal organization, but only to indicate the limits of this influence.

The Formal Function

The first function of the formal version of the organization is primarily legal. That is, reference is made to the formal version whenever some contractually binding activity is undertaken, or when there is dispute about legal matters. For example, reference is made to the formal organization when employees are hired or fired, or when employees are promoted or demoted, or departments or individuals are "moved" on the organizational chart.

The formal organization acts as a reference point for solving disputes, but the informal organization also plays an important role in solving disputes (see Ellickson, 1991). For example, if a secretary is fed up with the many tasks her boss expects her to do that are outside her official duties, she can pull out her formal contract and job descriptions to remind her boss what exactly her formal duties are in the company.

However, not all deviations from the formal organization are mistakes. On the contrary, in many cases such deviations are applauded as creative and time saving. For example, employees often find ways of doing the job first and getting approval on paper after an event, so that strategies are adopted and investments are committed before the paperwork authorizing them has gone through the appropriate channels. This kind of activity is seen as dynamic, although it is contrary to formal procedures and may be reproved by auditors.

The Planning Function

A second very important function of the formal organization is to act as a reference point, a commonly accessible construction of the corporation, during all planning activities.

Corporations invest a considerable amount of resources in the development of business plans, both long- and short-term ones. During such planning activities, the senior managers and other employees and consultants involved in planning bring with them their constructions of the organization, particularly its strengths and weaknesses. Such constructions are inevitably different across individuals and groups, sometimes fundamentally so. For example, we have witnessed senior managers of the same corporation disagreeing about issues such as the extent to which their company is top down or bottom up, or centralized or visionary, in leadership and homogeneous or diverse in corporate culture. It is inevitable that managers would develop different constructions of the corporation with respect to such characteristics.

To take another example, in the midst of a debate about how to direct R&D investments, market segments are selected on the basis of existing product and/or research strengths while one of the managers pulls out the formal organizational chart and point out how things are supposed to be. In this case, "supposed to be" points to the future oriented function of planning that must reflect opportunities and threats in the environment and not just strengths and weaknesses in the organization.

Past successes lead to the formation of unofficial power centers that ultimately influence decisions based on historic rather than future opportunities. Of course, such planning on the basis of past strengths can be illusory. For example, management may still be planning in the 1990s on the basis of particular R&D strengths the company enjoyed in the 1980s or even earlier, without giving adequate attention to new and different areas of strength now present in the company.

Because constructions of the corporation can differ, the formal version of the corporation can serve the function of an anchor. Claims based on the formal version of the organization are more tangible and can serve as common ground for future planning.

The Command Function

A third function of the formal organization is to establish command hierarchies, the chain of command, and to locate employees within the organization. The command function includes levels of responsibilities, task assignments, and reporting obligations, in hierarchical order from the top of the organization to lower levels. A purpose of command hierarchies is to facilitate project implementation.

The Functions of the "Unofficial" Organization

The unofficial organization consists of shared representations about the organization. These representations are discursively produced. They are constructed through the shared understandings of the employees and others who interact with the organization. They are thus social, being more than just the product of individual subjectivity (although individuals do have shared representations of an organization, some aspects of their representations are also uniquely personal). The informal organization has a set of functions that parallel those of the formal organization.

The Implementation Function

To get things done, an organization needs champions of causes who resolve conflicts, build alliances, and take initiatives and risks. Such champions make progress in multidisciplinary environments of interdepartmentally overlapping tasks. The job descriptions in such situations tend to nurture bureaucratic behavior, not necessarily because the job holders are bureaucrats but because the job descriptions often highlight functional goals or objectives for achievement. Such functional objectives are not directly relevant to product goals.

For example, a researcher in oncology working for a pharmaceutical company evaluates her own performance through publications in peer-reviewed oncology journals, rather than by speeding up the development of a new cancer drug that will be marketed by the company. Consequently, she may be a successful researcher but still not contribute effectively to the company. To label this oncologist's performance as "bureaucratic" may seem harsh, after all, she is an eminent researcher in her own specialty. However, as the term is used in organizational performance, bureaucrat means working within the pigeonhole of functional objectives rather than being sequentially integrated into product-related projects and goal achievements. The official organization with its classic job descriptions cannot cover these essential activities that are in essence contingent tasks and need to be managed as contingencies. For example, the discovery and development of cyclosporine (Sandimmune), one of the great successes in modern pharmaceutical history, was championed by researchers who clearly performed outside their formal functional corporate roles (Borel & Kis, 1991).

The Adaptive Function (vs. the Planning Function)

The formal organization lacks the flexibility required to respond adequately and speedily to the changing conditions of the market. A variety of interrelated and complex factors are involved in these changing conditions, including consumer demand, competitive strategies, technological innovations, economic fluctuations, and political and ethical trends. An example of such changing conditions is the health care reforms underway in North America and elsewhere, and their implications for the pharmaceutical industry. Drug development processes now have to integrate cost-benefit studies in addition to the standard documentation on safety, efficacy, and quality of life claims. The new demand for cost or price justification does not add anything to the therapeutic value of new drugs, but it has to be met because the new customers of the pharmaceutical industry (the health insurers, the institutional buyers in managed health care, etc.) require information about what value for money they will receive. It is the informal rather than the formal organization that can best respond to such changing demands, at least until the time comes when the formal organization can be revised to closer match altered market conditions.

The Identity Function (vs. the Command Function)

Another key function of the informal organization is to act as a source of social identity for individual employees. The demise of traditional institutions, such as the church, the family, and the local community, has meant that the work organization now plays a much more important role in the identity of employees. Relationships developed in the work setting come to have a central place in personal lives. In turn, the informal social networks that evolve, linking work and home, influence job implementation, morale, prestige, and motivation at work. This facilitates employees becoming effective outside their official functions.

Constructions of the Organization: Business "As Ifs"

The constructions of their organizations that employees have are often very different from the official version of the organization.

Cognitive Maps of Organizations

To clarify this point, we can conceive of each employee as having a construction of the organization he or she works for, just as each citydweller has a cognitive map of the city he or she inhabits (see Bell, Fisher, Baum, & Greene, 1990). Constructions of organizations will often be very different from the "official" organization, just as cognitive maps of cities deviate from the "official" map of the city.

For example, we asked employees to draw organizational charts, and to show the power of each manager by the size of the circle representing him or her. We also asked employees to show lines of command and communications between departments and managers. The result was very instructive: The organizational charts drawn by the employees reflected systematic differences between the representations held by respondents and the formal organizational chart.

The same effect is found when people are asked to draw maps of the city, or even their own neighborhood. The size of certain buildings are exaggerated, while others are minimized, and distances are magnified or reduced, showing variations in the constructions people hold of cities.

Tapping "As Ifs"

In another exercise designed to tap constructions of organizations, we asked a group of employees of an international organization to complete a list of sentences that began with stems such as:

(1) I behave as if business is . . .
(2) I plan in business as if . . .
(3) I organize myself in business as if . . .
(4) I predict the future in business as if . . .
(5) I relate to people in business as if . . .

The surprising result was that there was considerable variation in the way that these employees, all working for the same corporation, conceptualized business. Inevitably, some people do see business as "war" and do behave as if they are in battle, but there are many other ways of seeing business, just as there are countless variations of exactly who is doing the fighting, which group or person is the enemy, and what the war is really about.

Clearly, there are many ways of conceptualizing business organizations. Irrespective of how right or wrong these constructions of the world are, each person uses his or her own particular construction AS IF it were the correct one. Partly as a result of this, there evolve certain illusions about the control people have over organizational performance.

Illusions of Control

One of the goals of organizations is to achieve control over the business environment, so as to implement business programs more effectively. In order to increase their control, organizations develop and implement business plans. In several ways, the control that organizations believe they have is illusory.

Most important, it is an illusion of control for a number of reasons.
(1) To begin with, the construction of the organization held by planners tends to differ from the actual state of the organization.
(2) Their assumptions about causal relations in the business environment often prove to be wrong, not necessarily because they were incorrect to begin with, but because they failed to adapt to changing circumstances.
(3) They often fail to recognize the gaps between planned and actual implementation of projects. In evaluating their plans, organizations reconstruct situations and so reconceptualize their plans as being more successful. They also

revise their official plans and bring them closer to the socially constructed or informal organization. For example, what we read as successful business strategies are often actually *a posteriori* accounts, prepared after successful product launching.

Are There Limits to How We Remake Organizations?

Since all constructions of the organization must necessarily differ from the official version of the organization, would we be correct in assuming that there are no absolute criteria for evaluating performance in organizational settings? This assumption is invalid, because such criteria become apparent when we consider the minimal requirements necessary for organizational functioning.

To say that employees hold different constructions of organizations is not to imply that we can in practice design organizations in any way we like. There are certain very strong limits to how we can remake organizations. For an organization to function at all, a minimal set of conditions must be met (Holiday, 1988).

Trust

The first requirement is that people in the organization must be able to trust one another. This is not to imply that everyone in the organization must be trustworthy, because there will always be some individuals who are false and are generally not to be trusted. For example, Robert Maxwell survived for many years, even though he was untrustworthy. He seemed to have lied even to his own family. Some individuals will not fit this "trustworthy" norm. However, the norm of trust implies that the general rule followed by most people must be to be truthful, so that generally people can trust one another. An organization where the norm is for people to lie rather than to tell the truth would not survive very long.

Position Acceptance

The second condition for the survival of an organization is that employees generally accept the positions allotted to them, locating them both vertically and horizontally in the organization. For example, managers should accept the authority of the CEO, just as secretaries should accept the authority of managers. Also, employees should accept the departments and sections of the organization to which they are assigned. For example, employees assigned to marketing should not decide on their own authority to "move themselves" to research and development, or to report to the manager of the finance division rather than the marketing division. Without such general acceptance of the lines of command and departmental position, the organization would collapse.

Inherent in "position acceptance" is the assumption of responsibilities and rights of each position. For example, the positions of manager and secretary both have responsibilities and rights. Although in general managers enjoy more power than do secretaries, this does not mean that they can ignore the rights of secretaries.

However, we have emphasized that there only has to be general acceptance of positions, indicating that there need not be rigid adherence to the structure reflected in the official organization. There are many cases where the actual ways in which the organization functions suggest an organizational hierarchy and structure that is different from the official picture.

Common Understandings

The third requirement is that in order to function effectively, organizations must have common understandings, networks of ideas about correct behavior in the various domains of organizational life (this is similar to Edgar Schein's, 1985, notion of people in an organization having a psychological contract with those whom they take to be representatives of the organization). Examples of common understandings are ideas about correct behavior toward peers, superiors, and subordinates, as well as behavior during meetings, presentations, and performance evaluations. Each of these general types of common understandings indicates regular behavior patterns, repeated in very similar ways throughout the organization. For example, meetings regularly involve a select group of people, have set start and (less often) end times, are chaired by the most senior person present, follow a pre-announced agenda, are recorded in some manner, and so on.

The function of common understandings is to regulate social behavior and to make interactions within the organization much more predictable. In this way, communications can take place through a kind of "shorthand" so that employees spend less time and effort spelling out the details of each communication.

Concluding Comment

What is an organization? In answering this question, the general tendency has been for both laypeople and researchers to refer to formal organizational charts, formal objectives, and formal ways of doing things. The implication is that a high level of control is achieved by knowing the formal rules and pulling the appropriate power levers. In practice, however, the informal organization is often even more important in shaping how things are done in a particular firm. Control of the informal organization has proven to be far more illusive than control of the formal organization.

Critical Thinking Exercises

(1) What are the major differences between the formal and informal aspects of an organization? Why do the informal aspects make control difficult?
(2) Describe some limitations on how we could change organizations.

10

Controlling Corporate Culture

"Is it cutting edge?" asked the first man.

"No, definitely not," replied the second. "It's more `me too,' but warm and open. A lot of open doors and touchy-feely chats. How about yours?"

"Fast track, pushy pushy pushy."

"Top down I suppose?

"You bet, but now and again I put in an initiative, if I am sure the boss will like it. Only if I am sure, mind."

"I wouldn't like that culture. I prefer it warm and open."

The concept of corporate culture is now part of our language and the topic of our everyday conversations, as seen in the case of these two middle-level managers talking over a beer. Both laypeople and researchers now believe that corporate culture is relevant and important, particularly because it provides a means of controlling organizational change.

Control Through Culture

Since the 1980s the concept of corporate culture or organizational culture has become the focus of many leading thinkers in business. Culture (norms, rules, and values that prescribe "the correct way to do things here") became of interest because it seemed to be the key to better performance - something of vital importance in the competitive climate at the turn of the twenty-first century. Social scientists began to study the different cultures of corporations, just as they had much earlier studied exotic tribes in Africa and Asia and other distant places. A major concern was to identify those cultural features that made some corporations successful.

"Control through culture" became the leading slogan of many major corporations. It was assumed that through understanding and controlling culture, leaders would be able to control behavior in organizations. Following the corporate culture approach, there emerged reengineering, Total Quality Management (TQM), and other approaches to try to achieve the goal of increased control over behavior in organizations.

A Corporate Culture "School"

Although the literature on corporate culture is not as extensive as that of TQM or reengineering, it is based on more interesting theoretical ideas (see Deal & Kennedy, 1982; Frost & Moore, 1991; Ott, 1989), particularly in the case of Schein's (1985, 1992) analyses. We can refer to a corporate culture "school" in the sense that a clear viewpoint emerged from discussions on corporate culture.

The basic propositions of the corporate culture school can be summarized as follows:

(1) In each organization, there is a culture characterized by the norms, values, roles, and so on of the members of an organization.
(2) The cultures of organizations differ in fundamental ways. For example, some corporations have a top-down and others a more bottom-up management style; some corporations try to live up to being trend setters, others are more "me too" types.
(3) Corporate culture influences organizational performance, and is directly relevant to the bottom line.
(4) Corporate culture can be controlled through effective leadership.

Schein (1992) placed particular emphasis on the role of leaders in shaping organizational culture. His distinction between the primary and secondary mechanisms by which leaders influence change is useful; the first concerns the style or manner in which leaders do their work (this would include things like clothing, the way in which meetings are arranged and run, and, in general, how casual or formal the atmosphere is) and the second embodies procedures and rules (these are the formal guidelines about correct behavior).

The focus on "style" and other less tangible aspects of corporate life indicates that the corporate culture approach gives attention to the informal organization. Research in different cultures, such as the investigation of *guanxixue* (informal systems of obligations created by favors and gifts) by Yang (1994) in China, highlights the important distinction between formal and informal aspects of social relationships. It is becoming increasingly apparent that the informal aspects of organizations are important, and corporate culture does give attention to informal life. So far, however, the corporate culture approach has not had the same level of influence and status as TQM, or even reengineering, in the business world.

Multiplicity of Cultures in Each Corporation

The high expectations raised by the corporate culture theorists never came to fruition, perhaps in part because organizations have corporate cultures rather than just one culture each. Some of the cultures one can typically identify are an R&D culture, involving researchers motivated to achieve high status in the scientific community; a financial culture, with accountants and planners concerned with costs and profits; and a political culture associated with senior officers and board members, concerned to position the corporation correctly on the political map and keep shareholders and others happy (see figure 10.1). The corporate culture approach, then, is faced with the question, which culture is given priority?

A related point is that culture is dynamic and in a state of continuous change. These changes are often associated with the life cycles of corporations. The early history of successful corporations is often associated with rapid exploration and definition of roles and functions. The "identity" of the corporation takes shape in the minds of employees and the larger public. But in the turbulent climate of modern business, corporations often do not reach middle-age and stability. There is a constant possibility of mergers, takeovers, and other activities suddenly turning the world upside down. The "way things are down here" can suddenly become transformed into exercises of downsizing, reorganizing, and cost controlling.

In practice, then, corporate culture has proven to be elusive: There are many cultures in each organization, and each is continuously changing. Those seeking to control behavior in organizations have turned to other approaches.

The Total Quality Management (TQM) Approach

> The principal focus of a TQM organization is to provide goods and/or services that meet or preferably exceed the external (or final) customer's expectations in terms of functional requirements, value and cost.

> Thomas, *The Human Dimension of Quality* (1995, p. 185)

Total Quality Management (TQM) was developed with the purpose of managing the whole organization, while focus is kept on customer requirements (see Bowles & Hammond, 1991; Crosby, 1996; George & Weimerskirch, 1994; Hradesky, 1995; Juran & Gryna, 1988; McInerney & White, 1995). In 1987 the Malcolm Baldridge National Quality Award specified the most important elements that contribute to the quality of the end product: leadership, information and analysis, strategic quality planning, human resources development and management, management of process quality, quality and operational results, and customer focus and satisfaction.

One of the novel concepts incorporated in TQM is that each employee in the

IIX Corporate Culture and Illusions of Control

Subculture	R.& D.	Finance	Socio-economic	Political
Goals	Innovation	Shareholder value	Market share	Image
Assumptions	Scientific data and novel insights drive progress	Quarterly results reflect managerial performance	Documented cost-benefit means value for money	Opinion formation is a function of effective communic-ation
Constraints	Opinion leader consensus	Financial Return expected	Buyers' perception	Cultural trends

production process is both a producer and a customer. Accordingly, each employee should satisfy the requirements of other employees who are his or her immediate customers through a sequence of activities that have the requirements of the final customer, the consumer, as an end point.

The TQM approach is conservative, in that it leads to changes *within* the already existing formal structure of the present organization; it is a matter of taking what is already available and incrementally improving quality. Among the methods used to bring about change are greater employee participation, improved communication between departments, reorganized and increased specialization, and changes in process engineering.

TQM focuses almost exclusively on the formal organization, how things are supposed to be done according to the formal rules. Change is assessed on the basis of objective and quantified methods; and emphasis is placed on statistical methods, process flow charts, and procedures designed to maximize quantification. Of course, it is assumed that formal, rational, explicit organizational procedures are the most important in determining how well customer requirements are met.

The informal organization does not receive significant attention in TQM. Thus, the alternative culture(s) that often exists in organizations side by side with the formal culture is neglected. This leads to an emphasis on rationality and how things are supposed to work logically. Irrationality in organizations gets some attention (e.g., Thomas, 1995, part II), as does deviance and nonconformity (e.g., Bounds, Yorks, Adams, & Ranney, 1994, pp. 121-124). As a general rule, however, the informal organization is ignored in TQM.

Reengineering

> Business reengineering isn't about *fixing* anything. Business reengineering means starting all over, starting from scratch.
>
> Hammer & Champy, *Reengineering the Corporation* (1993, p. 2)

The book *Reengineering the Corporation* was intended to be a radical manifesto, and it is part of a reengineering movement that some see as revolutionary. This is certainly different from TQM and other approaches attempting "incremental improvement" in the organization. The proposal is to dismantle the entire organization and reengineer everything, even managers (see Champy, 1995).

Advocates of reengineering claim that complete change is necessary because of the fragmented and rigid nature of modern organizations. The tradition of Adam Smith, involving divisions of labor and hierarchical structures, should be swept away to make room for a more flexible system. There should be less specialization, better communications, and a more dynamic working system. Reengineering must be focused on key areas, such as business process, jobs and structures, management and measurement systems, and values and beliefs.

Like most revolutions, reengineering requires a change in the language people

use. As indicated by the term "reengineering," the new language is designed to give an impression of scientific precision. It is also designed to be more democratic, as supervisors become "coaches" and executives become leaders rather than "scorekeepers."

Assessing the Control Achieved

A major shortcoming of the TQM and reengineering approaches is a lack of attention to the informal organization. It is assumed that by controlling the formal organization, by attending to how things are supposed to be done formally, improvements can be made and efficiency increased. However, there is generally a gap, sometimes an enormous one, between how things are supposed to be done formally and how things are actually done, the informal way. This is a major reason why control has remained illusory for those adopting TQM and reengineering approaches.

Concluding Comment

It is now generally agreed that the culture of corporations is important for the bottom line. This realization has led to systematic efforts, through reengineering, TQM, and other procedures, to control corporate culture and to bring about changes in desired directions. But a major shortcoming of such efforts has been the neglect of the informal organization, the way things are actually done (rather than the way things are supposed to be done according to formal rules).

Critical Thinking Exercises

(1) Using a corporation that you know as an example, give examples of the formal and the informal ways of doing things.
(2) As long as we only see the formal organization, we can imagine that organizational cultural can be effectively controlled. Discuss this statement.

11

Leaders "In Control"

The Falkland Islands and their dependencies remain British territory.
No aggression and no invasion can alter that simple fact. It is the
Government's objective to see that the islands are freed from occupation
and are returned to British administration at the earliest possible
moment.

Margaret Thatcher, Speech to the House of Commons, April 3, 1982
(Thatcher, 1993, p. 183)

The "Iron Lady" perhaps best personifies strong leadership in modern times.
Central to this model is the assumption that the leader is in control. Indeed, in the
minds of many people taking control is synonymous with taking a leadership
position. Consider, for example, the image we have of Mrs. Thatcher's handling of
the Falklands crisis. When an Argentinean military force invaded and took over the
Falkland Islands on April 2, 1982, Thatcher's response was strong and unflinching.
She sent the British navy to war, justifying her actions on high moral, national, and
international principles. "We were defending our honour as a nation, and
principles of fundamental importance to the whole world - above all, that
aggression should never succeed and that international law should prevail over the
use of force" (Thatcher, 1993, p. 173).

British forces recaptured the Falklands quickly and decisively, and Thatcher's
account of the affair is full of Churchillian language, decorated with plenty of
phrases such as "standing firm." This kind of success in the face of adversity is
seen as an important hallmark of strong leadership, and accounts for the attention
given to "Churchillian leadership" by business managers, and described by Steven
Hayward in *Churchill on Leadership* (1997), among others.

Leadership is usually defined as a process by which a leader directs group
members toward the attainment of specific goals. The topic of leadership continues
to be of great interest to managers, because being a manager is in many ways seen
to be synonymous with being a leader (Kouzes & Posner, 1995; Mileham &

Spacie, 1996; Pincus & De Bonis, 1994). The main question addressed by researchers, often implicitly, has been, how can the manager best control employees and direct them to be more productive?

The many answers given to this question differ. Victor Vroom, for example, argued that participation in decision making best motivates employees, particularly those who are strongly independent and are egalitarian, as opposed to authoritarian (Vroom, 1960; Vroom & Jago, 1988). Fred Fielder proposed that how managers achieve control depends largely on their own style (Fielder, 1967; Fielder & Garcia, 1987). He distinguished between relationship-motivated leaders, who derive satisfaction from good personal relations with others, and task-motivated leaders, who derive satisfaction from successfully completing concrete tasks. Edgar Schein (1985) believed that managers can influence behavior in organizations through changing organizational culture, a set of unwritten assumptions about how people are supposed to behave. In the 1990s, there has been a renewed emphasis on participatory leadership and strategies through which group members can be influenced to feel more committed and loyal to the group (MacLegan & Nel, 1997). One thing has not changed over the years and remains common to the models developed by most management theorists, the assumption that successful leaders control the direction of the group. Indeed, some management theorists are explicit in claiming that managers can predict and control behavior (e.g., Drucker, 1954, 1987). On the surface, at least, this seems plausible. After all, what is an Iron Lady without the ability to control other people and events?

In this chapter we briefly consider a number of central ideas about leadership and dismantle the traditional model of "leader in control." The first part of our discussion is organized around four questions: Is leadership inevitable? Is leadership essential for effective group performance? Is leadership in the person or the situation? Is leadership both in the person and the situation? In the second part, we propose a new approach to leadership and suggest that leadership is not in persons or situations, rather it is in relationships. Using this new perspective, we reevaluate the topic of leadership and control

Is Leadership Inevitable?

Sometime in late March 1997, thirty-nine men and women, members of the Heaven's Gate cult, committed suicide in a California mansion. The suicides were carried out in an orderly manner in three stages, the first group helped was to die by the second group, and the second group by the third group. All thirty-nine bodies were dressed neatly and in an identical manner, and each had personal identification on or near it. The bodies were laid out neatly on beds, with suitcases by the beds. The mansion was scrubbed clean.

This incident was reported widely throughout the world, with each media source highlighting a different aspect of the story. Some tabloids focused on the discovery that some male cult members had been castrated and all cult members seemed to have rejected relationships and sex. Others gave more attention to the symbolic meaning and the wider implications of modern cults, such as the notion that cults represent a search for meaning in modern life. There was something common to all media reports: the assumption that the situation had been controlled by the cult leader, Marshall Applewhite.

The idea that leadership is inevitable is associated with the belief that societies are always characterized by inequality. In all societies, some people have more power and resources than others. This assumption is shared by a wide variety of thinkers, going back to Plato and other scholars in early Western history. In *The Republic*, Plato outlined the characteristics of the ideal society as he saw it. This ideal involved a three-tiered hierarchy, led by philosopher-kings who would be specially educated to fulfill their duties effectively. Plato's was a meritocratic system, requiring free movement of individuals in the hierarchy. Plato warned that if gifted individuals born to low-status parents are not allowed to rise up the hierarchy, and those of low ability born to high-status parents are not allowed to sink to a lower level, then the entire social system will collapse. The collapse of a hierarchical social system will lead to its replacement by another hierarchical system.

The inevitability of inequality is also emphasized by a wide variety of modern thinkers (see Taylor & Moghaddam, 1987). Jim Sidanius and others have explored the belief and value systems that help to uphold and legitimize inequalities in societies (Sidanius, Pratto, & Bobo, 1994). Although there are differences across cultures with respect to the details of these belief systems, the legitimization function they serve is the same for all cultures. Given this inequality, some individuals inevitably enjoy greater power to exert influence and to act as leaders.

Is Leadership Essential for Effective Group Performance?

Leadership seems to be universal and a "natural" feature of human societies. This certainly appears to be reflected in the way modern societies are organized. Business organizations have CEOs, labor unions have presidents, governments have prime ministers and ministers, sports teams have captains, even Mafia organizations have bosses, in just about every domain of human activity we consider, there is a leader at the head with more power and resources than other group members.

Some writers have argued that inequalities of power and resources are not only inevitable but are also essential if groups are to become effective. Sigmund Freud (1921) believed that the only groups worth considering are those with leaders because those without leaders are not able to act cohesively. Only through effective leadership, Freud argued, can groups become organized and directed in their actions. Essential roles of the leader are to displace negative feelings and thoughts onto outsiders and to help group members feel positive about themselves and the

group. Even Karl Marx acknowledged that leadership is essential to achieve collective action. For Marx, the proletariate revolution would be ignited and led by vanguards of intellectual activists who would generally be from outside the ranks of the lower classes.

Chairman Mao Tse-Tung (1893-1976) of China perhaps best represents the revolutionary spirit against group inequalities and power monopolies. The so-called cultural revolution he initiated in China in the late 1960s was directed against intellectuals and other groups of leaders who were "put in their place" and "reeducated" to keep in step with the (apparent) wishes of the masses. Ironically, Mao's actual style of behavior was a continuation of traditions set by emperors before him. Thus, he is aptly described as one of the "new emperors" (Salisbury, 1992).

Modern researchers have also highlighted the importance of the leader in collective action. Foremost among these are John McCarthy and Mayer Zald (1977), who have outlined resource mobilization theory, which proposes that social movements are largely influenced by leaders who control resources. From their perspective, feelings of discontent are only of secondary importance because they are always potentially available, they can be manufactured by those who control resources. Thus, it is not the "aggrieved" who initiate and direct collective action, but those with resources, who tend to be from outside the aggrieved group. An important example of this is the role played by the National Council for Senior Citizens for Health Care through Social Security (NCSC) in the movement to provide federally funded health care to the elderly in the United States. Most of the people active in the NCSC were young and middle-aged professionals, and funding came from the AFL-CIO. It was only after the direction and policies of the movement were in place that a broader base was sought and large numbers of the elderly population were recruited.

Is Leadership in the Person or in the Situation or Both?

Explanations of leadership have tended to shift between two extreme positions (see Northouse, 1977). The first is the "great person" model and assumes leadership to be in the person; the second is the situational approach that believes the requirements of a context "make" particular individuals into leaders.

The great person view owes much to the German sociologist Max Weber (1864-1920), who used the Greek term charisma to refer to any characteristic that sets the leader apart from other people (Weber, 1947). Modern researchers have treated charisma as a mystery quality that some leaders are supposed to have, (Kanungo & Conger, 1989). The assumption is that a leader with charisma would be a leader anywhere, independent of context. Churchill would have been a leader in any context, so the argument goes, because he had that unique quality that got other people to follow him.

A problem with the great person approach is that decades of research has failed to reveal a set of characteristics that are shared by leaders and not by others (Hogan, Curphy & Hogan, 1994). Perhaps this is because leaders in political, commercial, military, scientific, educational, and other domains have different characteristics and should not be compared. Maybe we should, instead, just compare leaders in one domain. Some researchers have tried this approach and claimed to have arrived at characteristics that are common to leaders in one domain, but not shared by outsiders (Kirkpatrick & Locke, 1991). A closer look at the findings of this research shows it to be simplistic and perhaps misleading. For example, two of the characteristics of successful business leaders are supposed to be trustfulness and honesty (Kirkpatrick & Locke, 1991). These are among the last traits we would ascribe to business leaders such as Andrew Carnegie, known for his ruthlessness and manipulation of other people - his workers, managers, and family members. The same could be said of Henry Ford and many other successful business leaders.

Taking a common sense approach, some researchers have proposed that leadership must be in both the person and in the situation. Contingency theory (Fielder & Garcia, 1987) is the most well researched example of this viewpoint. After decades of research, it is still not possible to pinpoint a set of characteristics in the person and the situation that is unique to leadership.

Given the poverty of explanations about leadership, we believe it useful to develop a completely new approach. Leadership is not in persons or situations, it is in relationships.

Leadership Is in Relationships

> So off they (the plant workers) go to try it for a couple of days. If it doesn't work, they can come back and tell us: `That's a bad idea. Here's a better way to do it.' The word gets around pretty quickly that management is listening, that we really care about quality, that we're open to new ideas, we're not just a bunch of dummies. That may be the most important consideration of all when it comes to quality - that the worker believes his ideas will be heard.

> Iacocca, *Iacocca* (1984, p. 185)

The legendary automobile manufacturer Lee Iacocca seems to be an example of the leader as great person. The son of Italian immigrants who arrived in America in 1902 with little money and even less knowledge of English, Iacocca appears to be yet another self-made person in the rags-to-riches tradition of the American dream. A careful study of his life, however, reveals a different picture. His parents arrived in America with something very precious: values and goals, such as giving priority to education, that were in line with those of the American middle class. Iacocca's success was in applying these values, but also in recognizing the primary importance of relationships for leadership success. The idea that workers should feel that their voices are heard is an indication of this recognition.

Relationships are dynamic and in a constant state of flux. They are not static and "given," as one might imagine the characteristics of a great person/leader or those of a situation to be static. Relationships are guided by how people interpret norms and rules, what they perceive to be correct behavior in a changing environment. In this connection, a useful concept is that of a psychological contract, which arises from the work of Edgar Schein (1985). A psychological contract is the unwritten set of expectations operating between individual employees and those who "stand for" the organization. A psychological contract is much more than formal contracts about pay and benefits; it concerns assumptions and expectations about status, dignity, pride, honor, and countless other aspects of social relationships.

The idea of leadership being grounded in relationships, rather than in persons and situations, is also implicit in the work of other writers. William Ouchi (1981) has highlighted relationships as the major factor leading to better performance in Japanese organizations, which involve more trust and intimacy between managers and workers than do Western organizations. Trust is not a quality of a manager or a situation, it is a feature of a relationship. To better understand relationships, we must look to normative systems.

Relationships evolve within the norms and rules of society. Such norms and rules specify correct behavior and correct relationships. Ouchi's (1981) research shows that in Japanese organizations, the norm of trust is powerful: It leads to trusting relationships. The expectation in Japanese corporations is for high levels of trust, but this is not so in American organizations. Of course, there are exceptions in both cultures. Some Japanese leaders will prove to be untrustworthy, just as some American leaders will prove to be trustworthy. Ouchi's important insight is that, for the most part, trust is higher in Japanese organizations than in American ones.

The difference between U.S. and Japanese organizations may not be so much in level of trust as in the motivation of employees. There is a greater tendency among Japanese employees to work with group consensus toward generally accepted objectives. This implies greater interdependence. Managers in the United States and (some other Western societies) tend to have more individualistic goals, as well as loyalties directly to the self rather than to the organization.

Relational Leadership: Implications

A relational view of leadership has a number of important implications. It implies that a major challenge for leaders is to build relationships and to give highest priority to the kinds of relationships achieved. This requires that target audiences be differentiated, in terms of interests, communication styles, and so on. For example, internal audiences for managers in a large organization might include scientists, finance managers, and subordinates. To achieve trusting relationships with each of these groups would typically require the manager to be influenced by different norms: the scientists value innovation and derive prestige through research breakthroughs; the finance managers keep their eye on the bottom line and are wary of risks involved with innovative ventures; and subordinates might value opportunities for greater participation in decision making.

Leaders are not able to control relationships absolutely, but they can affect relationships through influencing norms. The extent of this influence may be minimal, however. Norms of American society have shifted dramatically with respect to the correct behavior of politicians. In the 1960s, John Kennedy was able to enjoy extramarital affairs with various women, including Marilyn Monroe, but a shift in norms meant that Bill Clinton got into a great deal of trouble because of reported extramarital affairs. Clinton quickly came to be known as a president people could not trust. His behavior was no worse than Kennedy's, but the norms of presidential behavior had changed.

Concluding Comment

Leadership seems to be nearly universal. The idea that leadership means control, and that effective leaders are successful at controlling other people, is compelling. Hard evidence suggests that leaders do not have unique characteristics in common and that their influence on other people is largely dependent on situations. The best way to view leadership is in terms of the characteristics of relationships, rather than those of individuals or situations.

Critical Thinking Exercises

(1) Explain the great person, situational, and relational views of leadership.
(2) Being a leader means being in control of the formal organization, but not necessarily the informal one. In what ways is this true?

12

Modern Specialists: Greater and Greater Control over Less and Less

Estragon: Where shall we go?
Vladimir: Not far.
Estragon: Oh yes, let's go far away from here.
Vladimir: We can't.
Estragon: Why not?
Vladimir: We have to come back tomorrow.
Estragon: What for?
Vladimir: To wait for Godot.
Estragon: Ah! (Silence.) He didn't come?
Vladimir: No.

Samual Beckett *Waiting for Godot* (Act II)

Like the characters in a comedy-of-the-absurd play, specialists on the brink of the twenty-first century are in search of something that is always about to arrive, but never actually falls into their hands. It always seems that just a step ahead, just around the next corner, just over the next hill lies what increasing specialization is searching for: control. The ability to manipulate events and shape the future, a prized goal on the path of ever-increasing specialization (for a detailed discussion of increasing specialization and its consequences, see Moghaddam 1997).

The modern world is characterized by increasing specialization, in just about every conceivable domain. The move toward greater specialization is justified in a number of ways, mostly associated with the goal of increasing control. In this chapter, we shall review the various justifications for increasing specialization and assess the assumption that increases in specialization lead to increases in control. Our contention is that in most cases this assumption is misguided and that increased specialization actually leads to illusory control. That is, although modern specialists *feel* they are more in control, their ability to control future events is often actually diminished by their specialized outlooks. Modern specialists live in very narrow worlds, and their diminished visions lead them to exaggerate their own abilities to control events.

We begin by reviewing the economic rational for increased specialization. We believe this rationale has extended from the industrial domain to specialization in academia. We use the illustrative examples of environmental pollution and the organization of the work force on factory floors to illuminate how specialization has led to decreased rather than increased control. We conclude by discussing possible links between specialization and "personality" characteristics of specialists. Our proposition is that the mastery experts acquire in very narrow domains often leads to an illusion of control in the larger picture.

The Bottom Line: Economics, Increasing Specialization, and Control

The economic rational for specialization was first developed by economists of the eighteenth and nineteenth centuries, particularly by the father of classical economic theory, Adam Smith (1723-1790). Smith, a Scottish professor who first made his mark in the domain of moral philosophy, gave the fullest account of his economic ideas in his work entitled *The Wealth of Nations*, which first appeared in 1776. In order to appreciate the powerful impact of Smith's thesis, that "divisions of labor" act as the main source of increased production and wealth, we need to consider the historic context in which he wrote.

At the time *The Wealth of Nations* appeared, the Industrial Revolution was already underway in England and some other parts of Western societies. Within another century, industrialization had changed the economic, social, and political landscape of Europe. Millions of people had poured into rapidly expanding and industrializing urban centers. Mechanization of farming meant that farms became large-scale enterprises, needing fewer people per acre to work. The displaced farm laborers trooped into urban centers, to be transformed into urban dwellers and factory workers.

New sources of power, particularly steam power, meant that the factory could replace the home as the most important center of production. Home crafts and industries became economically inefficient. The main advantage of the factory, according to Smith, was that it could be organized to achieve greater divisions of labor. Smith's famous example of the pin factory became a classic case, recounted in most economic texts right up to present times. Smith described how a top-of-the-pin maker and a bottom-of-the-pin maker could produce more pins working as a team than if they worked independently to make whole pins. This is because through specialization each person could perfect a small task and also be more productive because, for example, no time would be wasted switching from task to task.

Increased production would mean that more goods would be available on the market, at a cheaper price. Consequently, there would result a "consumption gain." The whole society would become more productive through increased divisions of labor, and wealth would increase throughout the land.

Specialization Outside the Factory

Smith was mainly concerned with divisions of labor in the factory, and his discussions focused mostly on workers. At the same time the development of modern science was already leading to some specialization among researchers and various professionals, such as medical doctors. The ideal of the "Renaissance individual," the Leonardo da Vinci character who could move with ease from mathematics to engineering to medicine to philosophy, was still very much alive, but the leading scientific figures were to some extent specialized.

From the seventeenth to the early twentieth century, this specialization among researchers and professionals did not move rapidly, and the ideal of the Renaissance character persisted. Isaac Newton (1642-1724), the great English scientist and mathematician, and Albert Einstein, perhaps the twentieth century version of Newton, were both very capable of tackling philosophical issues well outside the particular scientific domains for which they gained their greatest fame. One could mention a number of other twentieth century figures, such as Bertrand Russell and Ludwig Wittgenstein, who showed superb insights into issues in diverse realms, including mathematics, philosophy, and psychology.

But during the nineteenth century, particularly after the 1860s, there emerged a different ideal, one associated with narrow specialization, a person who knew everything there was to know about a very specific topic. The emergence of this new ideal was based on the idea that because knowledge has expanded so rapidly, leading to a knowledge explosion and information revolution in the latter part of the twentieth century, one person cannot possibly know things in-depth over a broad area, and expertise can only come through very narrow specialization.

Rise of Modern Professions

The story of the rise of modern professions has been recounted in detail by a number of scholars, but we would like to highlight just a few aspects of this history. Although no single factor is uniquely responsible for the rise of specialized professionals, mainly in the nineteenth and twentieth centuries, two factors are worthy of particular attention.

First, to some extent increasing specialization among professionals can be explained by reference to Darwinian evolutionary theory. To use the terminology of this tradition, specialization among professionals to some extent stems from an attempt to identify and occupy vacant spaces (areas where resources are accessible

but that are not yet occupied by rival professionals). For example, by laying claim to a vacant space and labeling it "international aviation law," legal professionals can monopolize a set of vital resources. By establishing professional associations, specialized examinations and certification boards, and the like, these experts can limit the number of people having access to these resources.

Second, in some cases the development of specialized professionals represents an example of the "runaway evolution" we discussed in chapter 2. That is, the professional becomes more and more specialized and takes on characteristics that are actually not functional (just as the peacock develops feathers that have little function, except that they are preferred by females). However, the key requirement is that the "nonfunctional" specialization serves to attract customers, who are attracted to the specialized person and have the effect of perpetuating specialization among professionals.

The Famine-Wealth Cycle: A Challenge to Specialists

Smith's account of economic life was basically optimistic, and we may label him a "positive-thinking free marketer" in modern terms. He believed that increased divisions of labor and a free market system would lead to growth and prosperity for nations. From the beginning, there were a number of problems associated with the classic economics of Smith, and some of these were taken up by Thomas Malthus (1766-1834), David Ricardo (1772-1823), and others in this tradition.

One such problem concerned the rate of population increase, described by Malthus as being faster than the rate of increase in the food supply. The result is a cycle of famine and growth: as soon as the food supply catches up with population levels, people have more children, and this leads to another shortage and famine, then the rate of population increase declines, but very soon food supply catches up again, and the whole cycle begins anew. This seemed to be a situation that increases in divisions of labor could not solve because food supply was determined by limited resources, such as land availability.

Some have argued that the Malthusian cycle has been defeated by advancements made possible through exactly the kinds of specialization that Smith applauded. To take one example, modern birth control techniques developed by specialized medical researchers now allow us to control populations. Thus, in many Western societies the rate of population increase has been reduced to below or at 2.1 percent per annum (the rate needed to maintain population levels).

Specialized researchers have also helped to create the green revolution, using the application of modern genetic engineering and biotechnology techniques to dramatically increase food production and improve the durability of foodstuffs. Research has led to a new generation of seeds that are much more resistant to adverse weather conditions and natural diseases, and also have higher yields. Once the food is available, new technologies have increased durability; so that, for example, it is now possible to have tomatoes that sit on a shelf for six months and still remain fresh.

Other advancements that have helped to "break" the Malthusian cycle include large-scale social programs, such as health benefits and retirement benefits. These "insurances" help people to plan for their old age, without having to be dependent on their children to look after them. Thus, people now have control of their own lives.

Other thinkers argue that the Malthusian cycle has not been overcome and is very much with us today in various forms. For example, recent reviews of population growth reveal that we have not overcome the relatively fast rate of population increase and that food shortages continue in many parts of the world. The world population doubled between 1950 and 1990! During the last decade, world grain production has not kept pace with population increases, and famines are predicted in African, Asia, and elsewhere.

Modern experts have improved food production, but they have also decreased infant mortality and helped to increase the human lifespan. At one time a woman might become pregnant ten times, but only see four of her offspring grow to maturity. Now, however, it is possible to use birth control techniques to ensure that fewer pregnancies occur, but the children who are born will have a very high chance of surviving, and they will probably live longer.

Also, because of continued economic uncertainty in many parts of the world, children are still considered "insurance" for old age, children simply *are* the retirement package for people in many societies. Revolutions, corrupt governments, floods, earthquakes, economic disasters, and other such factors could lead to a collapse of welfare systems, but children can be counted on to look after their parents. By continuing this tradition, children know that they too will have such a retirement package when they grow old.

Thus, the expectation that increased divisions of labor would lead to increased wealth, and an escape from the clutches of the Malthusian cycle, has not been realized. Despite the apparent control we have achieved over production in industry and agriculture, and despite the predicted leveling off of population (which has yet to actually happen), the only predictions we can make with certainty is that there are going to be famines in some parts of the world and food shortages will continue.

One factor that might impact on this situation is changes in the farm subsidy systems of the European Economic Community (EEC), the United States, and Canada. Such farm subsidies act to keep the prices of foodstuffs higher than the level set by government-farmer agreements and, thus, prices are not lowered by the pressures of the free market system.

Expertise and the Sense of Control

One of the contradictions of modern specialization is that on the one hand specialists feel more and more in control of the narrow domains within which they specialize, but on the other hand their actual control over the larger world remains limited and may in some situations become diminished as a consequence of the technological changes they help to bring about.

Two areas that can readily serve as illustrative examples are the environment and the factory. In each of these cases, the research of ever-more specialized experts has led to technological advancements that, when brought together in the larger sphere, are a recipe for disaster. It is still not clear if in the long term we shall be able to survive our own tendencies toward self-destruction through environmental pollution.

Environmental Pollution and Expert Control

Increasing specialization has been particularly influential in creating modern industries. On the factory floor, in R&D, in all other areas of industry, specialization has been increasing, and the result is partly in line with Adam Smith's thesis of increased production and wealth. The very productivity that Smith foretold has also led to a number of detrimental consequences that were not part of his plan.

It is not clear how the free market system advocated by Smith would cope with the issue of environmental pollution (at this point, it may be worth mentioning that Smith spent the last years of his life as a government official responsible for administering exactly the kinds of trade taxes that he wrote against in *The Wealth of Nations*). Part of the challenge raised by the issue of pollution is that it has been difficult to predict the harmful side effects of many newly produced substances. A classic example is the case of asbestos, but there are thousands of drugs and health treatments that were judged to have no negative side effects at one time, but later were identified as harmful and even life threatening. For example, it was only after decades of popularity that breast implants came to be seen as a problem in the early 1990s, resulting in a financial settlement for the many North American women who had received certain breast implants.

Modern specialists are capable of using scientific research findings in biology, biochemistry, chemistry, genetics, and related fields to produce new products in health, agriculture, and many other areas. Unfortunately, they are not capable of predicting the diverse consequences these products may have. Pesticides have helped achieve higher crop yields in the short term, but their environmental consequences are only now becoming apparent. Many modern drugs are also likely to have-long term consequences that we have little knowledge about at the present time.

Control at Work

If one was to take a single person and a single work as a symbol of Marx's vision of the treatment of workers in capitalist societies, that one person would be

Frederick Taylor and that one work would be his book *Scientific Management* (1911/1964). Taylor's goal was to establish a scientific method of management, and by so doing achieve maximum control for the manager. In order to arrive at this goal, Taylor gave particular attention to job design. The objective of such job design was to transform workers into changeable parts that could be replaced rapidly like any other part of a factory production system.

Taylorism took Adam Smith's ideas about the advantages of divisions of labor very seriously and attempted to get full benefit of these (supposed) advantages. In so doing, Taylor developed a scheme in which the worker was transformed into a creature described by Marx: a commodity that could be bought and sold easily on the market, just like any other commodity. This would be achieved by designing jobs to be as narrow and simple as possible, so that a worker with little or no training could learn to do the job in a very short amount of time. Thus, replacability was maximized.

Taylor's scientific management was designed to maximize the control of managers, in part by standardizing the behavior of workers. By first breaking down a production process into the smallest bits of work possible and, then through detailed studies of each bit of work, management could arrive at the most effective way of doing that work. Interestingly, Taylor's analogy of what he schemed was a baseball team. Every little act by each player was studied, and every single element of the game of baseball was put under the microscope. Most important to Taylor was the fact that the coach had complete control over who did what on the field.

Obviously in Taylor's baseball team there was very little room for players to show initiative and flair. It was the coach/manager who would control everything, and presumably direct the team to victory through his orders.

Taylorism found its most influential practical expression in Fordism, the mass-production conveyer belt system put into place by Henry Ford. In Ford's automobile factories, two objectives were to design the narrowest possible job for each worker and to maximize managerial control. The workers would not even change their positions: a conveyer belt moving at a speed controlled by management would bring work to them and take that work away (in this way the speed at which they worked was also controlled). Because each worker had a very narrow job, such as turning a particular screw or putting on a door part, it was possible to replace workers instantly and not "waste time" training the replacements.

Even at its five-dollars-a-day best, Fordism had very limited possibilities. This is ultimately because experience has shown that when modern workers are placed in narrow conveyer belt-driven jobs, they do not perform as well as when they are in more open job situations where they can work as part of a team and actually show initiative. Thus, since the 1970s the team- oriented production approach of the Japanese, Swedes, and others has led to greater success and also been copied by automobile manufacturers in the United States.

To return to the baseball scenario so loved by Frederick Taylor, winning teams are ultimately those that have players with extraordinary flair, where the unusual and unexpected is attempted and achieved, and where the coaches give room to players to perform creatively. The managerial control dreamed of by Taylor would only lead to efficient production if workers were totally replaced by robots.

Control and the Personality of Experts

Little serious attention has been given to the relationship between the kinds of work people do and the impact of this work on their personalities. Of course, the general assumption on the part of many social scientists, including those influenced by Marx, is that the positions of people in the production process and their production roles are major factors influencing their consciousness and their social relationships. This thesis has exerted greater influence in Europe than in North America. A consequence is that this thesis never came under the full glare of empirical inquiry in the American tradition. Rather, it remained a thesis for theoretical discussion in the European tradition.

Work is such a major component in the lives of modern people that it seems certain that is does have a powerful impact on their behavior patterns and personality in general (Moghaddam, 1997). One of the characteristics of work on the brink of the twenty-first century is its specialized or narrow nature. This is particularly the case in research and some other professions. University professors now tend to be trained in narrow areas, and their Ph.D. students become trained in even narrower specialties. Each new generation of Ph.D.s gains expertise in a narrower domain than the previous one.

As the domain of specialty decreases in scope, the sense of control seems to increase. This is because the specialist moves deeper and deeper into a narrower and narrower groove. Thus, each generation of specialists has greater and greater command of a narrower and narrower domain.

Control of "Imperial" Specialist Domains

The trend toward diversification and increasing fragmentation in the specialties strengthens the feeling of control enjoyed by specialists. Associated with this process is the growth of organizational structures that, first, help support specialist activities; and second, act to increase specialization.

Organizational Structures and Specialized Activities

As new specialty areas develop, specialists active in each area establish organizations and various institutional structures to legitimize claim to, as well as to try to extend, their territories (vacant spaces). Cases in point are the many professional associations established by professional specialties (such as the

American Medical Association, the American Chemical Society, the American Psychological Association). In most cases, these associations serve a territorial function, acting very much like labor unions to protect the rights of members. For example, the American Medical Association regulates the total number of medical doctors available in the U.S. market by influencing the immigration and licensing of foreign-trained medical doctors.

The institutions associated with each specialization help to organize activities, such as conferences, seminars, and other research gatherings, where fellow specialists meet and exchange views with one another. These exchanges typically involve a closed group because only specialists in a specific domain attend. The main players are well known to everyone, as are the major values and taboos. By meeting with similar-minded specialists, it is possible for each group of specialists to maintain its view of the world.

Organizational Structures and Increasing Specialization

As the number of people in a given specialty increases, the competition for resources in that area also goes up. Consequently, pressure builds up for newcomers to find new vacant spaces. For example, as the number of lawyers specializing in corporate law increases, newcomers find it difficult to make a living because there are limited free resources (e.g., unclaimed clients) available. As a result, a new branch of corporate law is initiated.

Such initiation typically involves a series of steps, including the establishment of a new organization that reflects the more specialized interests. Also, there will be new publications and conferences on the more specialized topic. For example, during the 1980s and 1990s the new area of biotechnology represented a vacant space into which poured thousands of young Ph.D.s, moving away from such traditional areas as the biological and chemical sciences (with their sub specialties of microbiology, biochemistry, bioengineering, and the like). By the mid 1990s biotechnology was a fairly densely populated vacant space, with many international and national biotechnology organizations, biotechnology journals, and annual and biannual biotechnology conferences.

On the brink of the twenty-first century, it may already be that new science Ph.D.s will find the competition in biotechnology too fierce, and the pressure will be on them to discover fresh vacant spaces where there will be less competition for resources. The biotechnology industry in the United States, centered mainly in California, Boston, and Greater Washington, D.C., may have reached its maximum potential, and different industrial branches will emerge in the first decade of the twenty-first century. Although we cannot predict the direction of future development, it is very likely that new offshoots from the biotechnology industry will involve even more specialized researchers.

Concluding Comment

One of the consequences of researchers and professionals living and working within the confines of their own specialized world, of talking, thinking, eating, and sleeping in the company of other specialists in their own narrow areas, is that their peculiar view of the world is endorsed by those around them. They become masters of all their world, and even though this world is specialized and in most cases very narrow, they feel that they are in control. They become giants in a tiny land.

The professional associations help to make bigger and bigger giants, by giving awards to "great" researchers and "monumental thinkers." Despite the fact that in the vast majority of cases such "giants" are really very ordinary performers in very small domains, they are presented as "giants" and come to see themselves as giants. Within the minuscule domains they inhabit, at least, they come to feel they have control.

Critical Thinking Exercises

(1) Give examples of the pervasiveness of increasing specialization at work and elsewhere.

(2) Environmental pollution shows that the fruits of specialized know-how can spin out of control. Explain this statement.

13

Controlling the Economy and Other Great Illusions of the Dismal Science

Orthodoxy regards the economy as a complex, but nevertheless ultimately explicable and controllable, machine. There is an equilibrium path which the machine will follow, once the various component parts are serviced and in full working order. But on examination of the facts, this concept is not supported in the context of two key postulated relationships of macro-economics - between economic growth and employment/unemployment, and between unemployment and inflation.

Ormerod, *The Death of Economics* (1994, p. 151)

Will the discipline of economics survive to the year 2000? One inevitably asks this question after reading *The Death of Economics* (1994), in which the English economist Paul Ormerod seems to pull the ground out from under orthodox economics. Ormerod argued against the orthodox view of the economy as a machine, one that can be regulated and controlled in a predictable manner. This reminds us of the assumption inherent in mainstream psychology that individual humans are best conceived as thinking machines, and that the computer metaphor is the most apt one for human behavior.

Ormerod's critique was particularly devastating when he assessed two ideas central to economic orthodoxy. The first idea concerns the expectation that economic growth leads to a decrease in unemployment. The experiences of many developed world economies actually show that "a wide range of unemployment rates appears to be compatible with any particular average rate of economic growth over time" (Ormerod, 1994, p. 149). In other words, just because there is economic growth, it is not inevitable that unemployment will decrease. Observers of the United States economic scene during the 1980s and 1990s could add that the jobs that are created in times of economic growth need not be high paying. Indeed, since the 1980s most newly created jobs in the United States have been low-paying ones.

A second pillar of economic orthodoxy smashed away by Ormerod is the prediction that inflation increases with rises in employment. Once again, the actual experiences of developed nations suggest otherwise, so that "a wide range of inflation rates appear to be compatible with any particular path for unemployment over time" (Ormerod, 1994, p. 149). To take the example of the United States in the 1990s, although unemployment has been on or below 6 percent, inflation has also remained low, below 4 percent. Low unemployment has not led to increased demand for goods, and the expected increase in prices has not occurred. In fact, despite low unemployment and low interest rates, the U.S. housing market has remained sluggish, and *decreases* in prices have been reported in many parts of the country. A very similar trend is evident in England, in Canada, and in many other Western economies, even Switzerland.

"Amateur" Critics

It is not just professional economists such as Ormerod who are pointing out the lack of predictability in economic life and weaknesses in economic orthodoxy. For example, as we write this chapter, the business section of *The Washington Post* included an article by James Glassman under the heading, "You can't make heads or tails of the Dow," in which we read:

> Between Thanksgiving and last Wednesday, the Dow Jones industrial average rose 700 points - up, up, up at an inexorable 45-degree angle on the charts. Then, Thursday, the Dow fell 82 points. Why? The truth is that no one knows - just as no one knows why the Dow fell 509 points on Oct. 19, 1987. (May 21, 1995)

Glassman then pointed out that "ignorance" rarely prevents experts from putting forward "confident" explanations. For example, one pundit explained the latest fall of the Dow by explaining to Glassman that, "the number one worry is the sustainability of earnings and how strong the economy is" Glassman commented, "Huh? For months, pundits have been saying the market thinks a weak economy is good. Now it's bad?" In conclusion, Glassman stated that "there's a good case to be made that the movements of the stock market - and, more important, of individual stocks - are essentially random."

Random?!? Then what exactly are all of those financial/economics pundits paid to do? Perhaps the movement of stocks are not random, but rather like an out-of-control pendulum, moving too far to extremes. The main point here is that the "experts" attempt to portray a predictable and controllable picture of events.

We find a similarly critical tone toward economic orthodoxy when we open up European newspapers. For example, the generally conservative *Neue Zurcher Zeitung*, the leading Swiss newspaper, published in the same period as the previously cited *Washington Post* article a critical discussion on economic forecasting (May 27/28, 1995). The article pointed out that economists have failed to predict such spectacular economic events as the crash of the Mexican economy and the changing fortunes of European interest rates and the U.S. dollar in the 1990s. The moral of the story, according this article, is that although economic forecasting often misses the mark, we have to stick to it because there are no alternatives.

Frontstage and Backstage of Economic Orthodoxy

While critics point out that economic orthodoxy is in trouble, this is very far from the impression one gets from reading Paul Samuelson's now classic book *Economics* (Samuelson & Nordhaus, 1992), or Micheal Niemira and Philip Klein's (1994) popular text *Forecasting Financial and Economic Cycles* (in which they confidently tell us how to predict inflation, interest rates, and stocks!), or any other "standard" economics text for that matter. The respectable face of economics is presented in such publications, and this respectability seems to be enhanced by mountains of mathematical models - such as those found in Adam Ostaszewski's (1993) *Mathematics in Economics* and James Friedman's (1990) *Game Theory*. (In psychology, also, complicated statistical procedures are imported to add respectability to the work of psychologists. Such statistical procedures camouflage what are sometimes wrong premises. Once again, we are reminded of commonalities linking orthodox economics, orthodox psychology, and orthodox versions of other social sciences.)

When we peep behind this curtain, however, we find the world backstage to be very different from what is presented frontstage. To begin with, human beings are not the rational creatures they are assumed to be by the vast majority of economic models. The rational pleasure-seeking creatures who participate in the games described in gaming theory do not exist on planet Earth, and perhaps they never did, or will, exist anywhere.

The Centrality of Prediction and Control in Orthodox Economics

Much has been written and said about the rift between liberal and conservative positions on economic issues. For example, conservatives believe that people are materialistic and rational in pursuing their self-interests. Given the freedom to pursue their individual ends, people will behave in a way that maximizes economic benefits for themselves and, ultimately, for society. Thus, the conservative American economist Milton Friedman argued in his influential book *Capitalism and Freedom* (1962) that all social organization should be arranged to allow

individual freedom because this will result in public good. In contrast, the great liberal economist John Maynard Keynes stated,

> It is *not* a correct deduction from the Principles of Economics that enlightened self-interest always operates in the public self-interest. Nor is it true that self-interest generally *is* enlightened; more often individuals acting separately to promote their own ends are too ignorant or too weak to attain even these. (Keynes, 1963, p. 312)

These differences in perspective between liberals and conservatives on the issue of individual freedom are pivotal and lie at the root of many other differences, such as ideas on government intervention. Liberals argue that governments must intervene to direct economic development, through influencing such things as taxation levels, interest rates, and public expenditure. From their perspective, the economy is a machine that needs a strong-minded engineer to direct its actions.

Conservatives, on the other hand, believe that the "economic machine" will run best if left alone, and that government intervention will only makes matters worse. In the conservative world, any control and direction that is required should come not from government, but from captains of industry. In this viewpoint, the economy is a self-regulating machine, and any adjustments that it needs will be made by those (captains of industry) who are part of the machinery. In this scenario, captains of industry act as thermostats, safety valves, and automatic feedback loops to keep the machine running smoothly.

Liberal and conservative viewpoints have in common the assumption that the economy can be predicted and controlled. Both orthodoxies believe that the machine is rational, and that it will go down tracks laid out for it - either by government intervention or by captains of industry acting without government interference. Let us take a closer look at this assumption by considering another aspect of economic life, time spent for work and leisure. We shall see that when it comes to the prediction of even very "simple" issues, such as the allocation of time for work and leisure, the future is never predictable or controllable.

It is particularly revealing to study the topic of leisure, because how much time we spend at leisure rather than at work is critical for economic life. As we shall see, "what" we do during our leisure hours is also crucial.

The Predicted Increase in Leisure Time

> "Why is a raven like a writing-desk?"
> "Come, we shall have some fun now!" thought Alice. "I'm glad they've begun asking riddles - I believe I can guess that," she added aloud.
> "Do you mean that you think you can find out the answer to it?" said the March Hare.
> "Exactly so," said Alice
> "Then you should say what you mean," the March Hare went

on.

"I do," Alice hastily replied; "at least - at least I mean what I say - that's the same thing, you know."

"Not the same thing a bit!" said the Hatter. "Why, you might just as well say that `I see what I eat' is the same thing as `I eat what I see'!"

"You might just as well say," added the March Hare, "that `I like what I get' is the same thing as `I get what I like'!"

Lewis Carrol, *Alice's Adventures in Wonderland* (1965, p. 70-71)

When we review discussions held over the last century on leisure time and predictions about how the working day would become diminished, we should be forgiven if we feel we have joined Alice, the March Hare, and the Mad Hatter in a tea party. The ordinary world is turned upside down, and we can never be sure we are standing the right way up.

From one viewpoint, the situation seems simple enough. Technological advancement means that machines replace people in doing many different tasks. In the home, for example, washing machines can wash our clothes, and dishwashers can clean our dishes, and lawn mowers can cut the grass in our yards, to mention just a few labor-saving devices. Even more fundamental changes have come about in the workplace, where modern robotics have allowed entire factories to become almost fully automated. In such modern factories, many of the routine tasks traditionally carried out by workers, such as drilling holes and assembling car parts, are now carried out by automated machinery.

Industry is becoming more and more automated and production of goods is also increasing, which means that employees as a whole will need to spend less time at work in order for the economy to achieve the same level of production. In the agricultural sector, also, fewer workers will be needed to produce food, as farming becomes more and more mechanized.

From the earliest stages of the Industrial Revolution, the idea that machines will replace people at work was interpreted in rather simplistic ways. Some groups of workers even took up arms against new technologies and set about smashing the machinery that was revolutionizing factories, beginning at the end of the seventeenth century. Such machine breaking became a well-orchestrated activity among the Luddites, English textile workers who organized riots against mechanization between 1811 and 1816. Others saw the introduction of the machine as more beneficial, because people would now be able to spend more time at leisure and self-improvement.

Events in the early twentieth century seemed to validate the view that more machinery means less hours of work (for further discussions of how automation was supposed to increase leisure, see Cross, 1994; Hunnicutt, 1989). This era witnessed the expansion of mass production systems, pioneered by Henry Ford and other American industrialists. New technologies led to enormous increases in productivity, but there were not enough jobs for everyone. Partly in an effort to get more job sharing, in 1933 the United States Senate passed the Black Bill, which mandated the thirty-hour workweek, the shortest workweek in U.S. history (both authors would like personally to practice the Black Bill, preferably in the South of France). The stage seemed to be set for shorter workweeks and more automation.

World War II dramatically changed the situation because the war effort required much longer working hours for almost everyone. Leisure became a secondary concern, as both men and women got used to working fifty, sixty, or even more hours each week. By the 1960s, however, it was fashionable again to talk about the "coming age of leisure." Predicting a revolution in work and leisure, Riva Poor and other experts (references to a good selection of these experts can be found in Poor, 1970) described how workers in industrialized societies would enjoy a three- or even four-day weekend (again, both authors would like to hear from employers ready to give them such options). During the 1960s and 1970s, there was a boom in leisure studies at universities, and academics became more interested in how people spent their leisure time. There was even concern that the general population was not adequately prepared to cope with all the leisure time that they would soon enjoy.

When we examine the actual pattern of work and leisure in modern societies during the last few decades of the twentieth century, we find that despite increases in automation and production, there has not been a increase in leisure time. Indeed, if anything people are working longer hours now. (We should not allow the growth of the tourist industry to fool us into thinking otherwise. The tourist industry boom is the result of transportation and communications revolutions, more retired people with money, and other factors, but not a decline in the number of hours worked by Americans.)

The Discovery of the Overworked American

When Juliet Shor (1992) examined the work and leisure trends of workers in the United States, the outcome was a book entitled *The Overworked American* rather than *The Leisured American*. Shor pointed out that Americans are working longer hours, and sacrificing personal and family lives, as they run, run, run to do more and more work (interestingly, Shor's important contribution was largely ignored in the United States).

What went wrong? Why did the predictions of a three-day week not come true? One explanation seems to be that the basic assumption that technology frees people was wrong. In some cases, technology created more work, particularly for the middle-class. For example, during the nineteenth century many middle-class households would send their clothes to be washed by professional services outside the home, but the introduction of the washing machine in the home meant that the middle-class housewife now had to do the laundry herself.

A more profound reason why increased automation and production did not lead to increased leisure time is that people experienced rising expectations. A culture of consumerism spread, leading people to want more and more consumer goods, so that they have to work more and more hours to earn money to purchase additional goods. Research suggests that, whereas during some earlier times in Western societies laborers worked only as long as they had to in order to maintain their standard of living, now workers want more and more, and have to work more and more hours to participate in the consumer society (Shor, 1992, provides historical examples of workers in the fourteenth century and other eras who were only interested in maintaining certain basic standards, rather than accumulating more and more).

We have now reached a stage where consumerism is itself a leisure activity. People work to earn money, and then spend their leisure time purchasing more goods with the additional money. Shopping has become a favorite pastime, a means of enjoying oneself and overcoming depression.

Part of this consumerism involves changing jobs the way we change cars, in what Rosabeth Moss Kanter has referred to as a shift from climbing to hopping in career strategies (see particularly Ch. 11 in Kanter, 1989). People are no longer content to remain in the same organization and try to work their way up the corporate ladder. In the new pluralism, employees have far less job security, but they have also discovered the benefits of a new mobility. Peter Drucker pointed out that, "even in Japan, despite the tradition of 'lifetime commitment,' knowledge workers now have increasing mobility as long as they observe ritual courtesies" (1989, p. 95).

The new norm of hopping from one job to another adds to the uncertainty and unpredictability of economic life. On the one hand, companies create feelings of instability among employees through streamlining, mergers, and other changes designed to cut costs and increase profits. On the other hand, employees job-hop more in order to stay ahead of downsizing and other changes that might ax their own jobs.

A Change of Direction?

> The general perception that the U.S. economy is in relatively good
> shape . . . reflects a kind of revolution in what Americans expect of their
> economy - a revolution of falling expectations.
>
> Krugman, *The Age of Diminished Expectations* (1990, p. 148)

The American economist Paul Krugman has argued in his recent book *The Age of Diminished Expectations* (1990) that Americans have stopped expecting their economic conditions to continually improve. Krugman pointed out that since the 1980s, many Americans have not experienced a rise in real income, and that in the 1990s many people are just happy to hold on to their current standard of living. Although this is an interesting interpretation of trends, it raises some concerns about the ways in which economists conjure up explanations for events.

In order to explain why working hours did not decrease as automation increased, economists referred to rising expectations. Now, in a situation where working hours and productivity have both increased, we are told that we have entered an age of diminished expectations. We are left wondering, which is it people are supposed to be experiencing - rising or diminished expectations?

A Paradox in Expectations?

Perhaps our era is best referred to as the "age of mixed expectations," when expectations are both rising and diminished. They are rising, in the sense that we continue to demand more and more consumer goods - changing our clothes, cars, furniture, accessories, and even jobs and homes, as often as possible. We derive deep feelings of satisfaction and security from playing the role of consumer.

On the other hand, our expectations seem to be diminished in two key respects. First, fewer people seem to expect stability and security in employment. Over the course of their working life, more people now believe they will have to work for a number of different employers, and perhaps even in different specialties. Second, in general we have abandoned the idea that our leisure hours will increase over the course of a career. If anything, we have now gotten used to the idea that we must work longer and longer hours if we are to enjoy real increases in our standard of living. This is particularly true for people in the third world.

Third World Economies and Debts

> Sovereign nations don't go bankrupt.
> Walter Wriston (quoted in Krugman, 1990, p. 143)

Events since the 1970s have shown Citibank's Walter Wriston how badly economic predictions can go wrong, particularly in the third world context. During the 1980s one third world country after another found it very difficult or, as in the case of Mexico, even impossible to repay its international debts. The crash of the Mexican economy in the early 1990s forced President Clinton to put together a $20 billion loan package, in the hope that the Mexican economy could be jump-started again. However, it is not at all clear whether such infusions ultimately serve to make third world economies sicker or healthier. Paul Krugman states the problem: "Countries are failing to work their way out of the debt problem because of slow growth; and they are growing slowly at least in part because of their debt" (Krugman, 1990, p. 148).

Concluding Comment

What lessons can we draw from the "Tequila shock" caused by collapsing Mexican and other third world economies in the 1990s? One possibility is that our orthodox economic formulas have much more limited applicability than we imagined.

When we look back over the last fifty years, it appears that our formulas for third world economic development have not been successful. Despite what seems like an obvious lack of success, we continue to show optimism and to rationalize our failures. This situation reminds one of what the American economist John Kenneth Galbraith (1994) had to say when he reviewed fifty years of personal experience in his book *A Journey through Economic Time*: "A certain political and economic correctness requires us to assign some measure of purpose, of rationality, even where, all too obviously, it does not exist" (p. 14).

One lesson we might learn from the "Tequila shock," then, is that our continued rationalization of failures can act to hinder our progress. We must nurture the courage to admit our limitations more openly.

Critical Thinking Exercises

(1) The idea that the economy can be controlled by economists was tested and found wanting in the experience of the USSR. Politicians in the West should take note. Discuss this statement.
(2) Give examples of the predictability and unpredictability of the economy.

14

Controlling Authoritarianism: Can We Survive Destructive Personalities?

When I was a young woman at university, back in the late 1920s, there was economic depression and a lot of suffering, but at least we thought we had the solutions. Everyone seemed to agree about the solutions . . improved standard of living, better health care, and most important of all the spread of science and education. We really believed science and education would solve political problems. But then came Hitler! I remember asking myself, how could this happen in such an advanced industrial society? Why did education and science not save Germany from hatemongers and fanatics? And now, after the bomb explosion in Oklahoma, I wonder if science and education can save America.

Eighty-nine-year-old American

The Oklahoma City bombing is Act II of the Waco tragedy.
Letter from Jerry A. Worley to *Time* magazine (May 29, 1995)

At the beginning of 1995, the world's two economic giants experienced unexpected shocks: the March 20 sarin gas attack on the Tokyo subway in Japan, and the April 19 bomb explosion in Oklahoma City, in the United States. These were not just physical attacks, they were also psychological bombshells. They led people to question their personal faith in progress. How could such primitive acts of violence occur in technologically advanced societies? Why did advances in science and education not make societies immune from fanaticism?

Members of the older generation, those who have personal memories of World War II, recall having been troubled by similar questions during much earlier times.

The horrifying events of World War II came as both a surprise and a great disappointment to people who assumed that modern industrial societies had advanced beyond war and genocide. The terrible atrocities committed during this and other modern wars, including the war in Vietnam, have been at the hands of the most "advanced" nations, using the most sophisticated technologies. When we look closely at this situation, a puzzling paradox appears. On the one hand, the liberal assumption that the spread of education and advances in science and technology will end prejudice and fanaticism seems to be strong still, and perhaps is becoming even more influential. Education, we tend to believe, will solve our problems and eradicate authoritarianism. On the other hand, we have not seen an end to intergroup prejudices (racism, sexism) or fanaticism in educationally and technologically advanced societies (for reviews, see Bowser, 1995; Lott & Maluso, 1995). Indeed, the country that first landed humans on the moon is also arguably ahead of everyone else in terms of ethnocentrism.

Most of us continue to have faith that science will solve our inhumanity to one another. Wordsworth asked, "Have I not reason to lament what man has made of man?" (in the poem *Lines Written in Early Spring*, 1798). Most of us agree he had reason to say this, but we remain optimistic that education will solve the problems. Science will unearth the roots of our inhumanity, and education will enable us to avoid historical pitfalls, such as war.

This faith is so strong that immediately after World War II, researchers launched major scientific studies designed to find out more about the roots of our inhumanity. By the early 1950s, the results of these studies were being published and widely discussed. The American scholar Gordon Allport reviewed a great deal of this research in his classic book *The Nature of Prejudice*, which first appeared in 1954, and it is telling that Allport restated the faith of these researchers and so many other people in science. In the preface to his book, Allport (1954) affirmed that:

> Especially encouraging is the fact that in recent years men in large numbers have become convinced that scientific intelligence may help us solve the conflict. Theology has always viewed the clash between man's destructive nature and his ideals as a matter of original sin resisting the redemptive process. Valid and expressive as this diagnosis may be, there has been added recently the conviction that man can and should employ his intelligence to assist in his redemption. (Allport, 1954, p. x)

But Allport and many others failed to bring into the open a paradox concerning science and humankind's destructive nature. Science has made tremendous strides in the twentieth century, but this has not prevented us from expressing our destructive nature. Indeed, science has allowed us to become far more effective in persecuting, torturing, and killing our fellow human beings. Evidence put forward in books such as The Breaking of Bodies and Minds (Stover & Nightingale, 1985) and in countless human rights reports at the turn of the 20th century clearly shows that advanced technology is used by modern governments to torture political prisoners, and the destructive potential of modern nuclear weapons is all too well known to require elaboration. In this and the next chapter, we examine illusions in two important but controversial domains: the control of authoritarianism and of war. Both chapters critically consider the illusion of control underlying the assumption that science and education will allow us to control our destructive tendencies.

Our Destructive Actions: Their Common Core

The scope of the discussion in this chapter is authoritarianism and the destructive tendencies with which it is associated. Authoritarians are potential fascists, in the sense that if a Hitler-style leader emerges, authoritarians are most likely to give support to such leadership and uphold the antidemocratic regime to which it leads. Authoritarians are prone to take part in radical and fundamentalist movements, to hold prejudiced attitudes, and to discriminate against minorities. Examples of this tendency range from refusing to hire job candidates because of their race to throwing bombs at people because of their religious convictions; from voting against a candidate for political office because she or he is female to shooting a person because of what she or he has written or said; from refusing to rent a house to a person because of her or his religious affiliation, to stabbing a person because of her or his political beliefs.

Seeing Is Believing: Ways of Seeing the World Associated with Destructive Tendencies

Over the last fifty years a vast mountain of social science research has helped to uncover some of the characteristics associated with authoritarianism. The landmark studies were conducted by a group of researchers in California immediately after World War II, and published under the title *The Authoritarian Personality* (Adorno, Frenkel-Brunswik, Levinson & Sanford, 1950). More recently, the Canadian researcher Bob Altemeyer (1981, 1988) developed a more sophisticated but perhaps also more narrow research program designed to unravel the complexities of right-wing authoritarianism.

What this research reveals is that central to authoritarian characteristics is a particular worldview, a style of categorizing the world and relating to the groupings that arise.

Authoritarians tend to have at least six important characteristics in common with respect to how they perceive the world.

(1) *The World Is Made Up of "Us" and "Them"*
A first feature of this worldview is a clear demarcation of the world into "us" and "them." The tendency to categorize the social world into "us" and "them" is universal. The complexity of the social environment leads us to use social categories in order to cope with the vast amount of information available. We also

generalize about members of social groups and arrive at stereotypes based on traits, reiterating statements such as "Italians are lovers," "French are great cooks," and so on. In recent years, researchers have come to recognize that stereotypes are not necessarily good or bad. They are simply functional; like any other heuristic device, they allow us to take shortcuts in thinking about the world (for a review of social categorization and stereotyping, see Devine, 1995).

Clearly, then, we all categorize the world and even use stereotypes of different groups. What are the special characteristics of people who behave in a destructive manner, those who hold very prejudiced attitudes, discriminate against others, and even physically harm or kill others because of racial or religious or political group memberships?

A first characteristic of such people is that they literally perceive the world in black-and-white terms so that the social categories they use have much sharper boundaries. Also, they seem to be more concerned about keeping their group separate. These points are illustrated in research studies where respondents are shown ambiguous photographs of faces and asked to identify the racial group to which each face belongs (see Taylor & Moghaddam, 1994). Respondents who are more prejudiced tend to be more cautious about including faces in their own group. Their working motto seems to be, "If unsure, exclude others from our group."

(2) *"We" Are Good and "They" Are Bad*

At the turn of the century, William Sumner (1906) published his important work, *Folkways*, in which he described what seems to be the universal tendency of "ethnocentrism." That is, wherever one looks in the human world, people seem to regard their own ways as the natural ones, their own beliefs and values as the correct ones, and their own kind as the superior one. Within their own group they share peaceful relations, but toward outsiders they wage war.

Perhaps the tendency to see the "out-group" as all the same, out-group homogeneity, is to some degree present among the normal population, but authoritarians exaggerate this trend. They see out-group members much less as individual persons, and much more as an indistinguishable mass, a homogenous machine. This tendency justifies treating out-group members in inhuman ways.

(3) *We Had Better Get Them First!*

What is the motivation underlying intolerance, hatred, violence, and generally destructive tendencies toward others? Can we identify the main motives? One highly likely candidate as a motive is defensive and arises from the perception of the world as a place full of threats.

The source of such threats could be immigrants, who are seen as taking away our jobs, ruining our way of life and traditional culture, trying to steal our women, spreading germs and diseases, and so on. Other sources are gays, artists, and other "deviants" who are seen to be a threat to the "moral mainstream." All such out-group members come to have what Erving Goffman (1963) refered to as "spoiled identities"; they become stigmatized.

Regardless of the exact identity of the groups seen to be a threat, the solution is clear: attack them before they have a chance to get us! They are sure to try to hurt us, so we are justified in doing it to them first!

This kind of "get the first punch in" thinking is also characteristic of people described by Richard Christie and Florence Geise (1970) as "high Machiavellians." These researchers used Niccolo Machiavelli's *The Prince* as their starting point in developing a measure of the personality trait "Machiavellianism." Individuals who score high on this trait are more likely to see the world as a threatening place, believe that some others are out to get them, and think that the safest strategy is to hit out first before others have a chance to attack.

A very important common feature of authoritarian and Machiavellian thinking is its conspiratorial nature; that is, the world is seen as multilayered, with hidden conspiracies being behind even everyday events. Of course, authoritarians have a greater tendency to see various outsiders (such as Jews, immigrants, or gays) as being behind the conspiracy.

(4) *All Is Fair in Love and War: The Ends Justify the Means*

Authoritarians generally act on the belief that the ends justify the means, at least as far as their own actions are concerned. Their reasoning goes something like this: given that "they" are out to get "us," and are constantly plotting and conspiring, then "we" are perfectly justified in using every available means to fight and to defeat "them." After all, our goals are right and just, and anyone opposing us in our march toward such goals deserves it if they are hurt or even killed. This kind of viewpoint can even lead to the justification of terrorism and bloody violence against civilians, as we saw in the recent bombing of the World Trade Center in New York.

(5) *Punitive Attitudes toward the Weak*

Authoritarians are punitive toward minorities and the weak, who they generally treat with disdain in both word and deed. They express negative sentiments toward minorities and are prone to discriminate against them when opportunities arise.

This negative disposition is not exclusively focused on any particular minority but is generalized to include many minorities. Thus, for example, they do not just hate blacks, but also Jews, gays, and others in minority status. Their targets, then, tend to be those who are weakest and most vulnerable in society.

(6) *Subservience toward Authority*

In contrast to their disdain for those whom they see as being below themselves, authoritarians are very submissive toward authority figures and generally those whom they see as being strong and above themselves. This was demonstrated experimentally by Stanley Milgram, who showed that authoritarians are more likely to follow the commands of an authority figure to administer deadly levels of electric shock to an innocent victim.

Thus, authoritarians show enormous respect for officials in the army, the church, and government. This subservience and loyalty to authority figures makes authoritarians more willing tools in dictatorships and repressive societies than people low on authoritarianism.

A Liberal Bias?

A careful look at the literature on authoritarianism reveals what seems to be a liberal bias, and this is most clearly seen in the work of Bob Altemeyer. For example, in his prize-winning book *Enemies of Freedom* (1988), Altemeyer built on his thesis that authoritarians are politically right wing. The profile of authoritarians in the West seems to fit this description as they are typically more religious, more conservative in their social views, and less educated than most.

However, when we examine this issue in an international rather than only a Western context, we realize that authoritarians are not exclusively rightwing, they could also be politically leftwing. For example, consider events in the former USSR since the 1920s. A strong case could be made for the view that Stalin and his followers were both leftwing and authoritarian. Also, the left-wingers who want a return to the "old days" even after the collapse of the USSR have the xenophobic hallmarks of authoritarians (see figure 14.1).

A very important but rather subtle assumption underlies the tendency of Altemeyer and other researchers to see authoritarians as rightwing. This is the assumption, seldom made explicit, that we shall be able to control authoritarianism through liberal programs that move society to the left of the political spectrum. It is implied that such a move will result in less religious and racial intolerance.

Authoritarian Illusions

> Fanatics have their dreams, wherewith they weave
> a paradise for a sect.
>
> John Keats (1795-1821) The Fall of Hyperion

Authoritarians find it particularly easy to believe in a paradise set up as a utopian goal. Such a paradise may be something to be achieved on earth, such as a classless society or a society of free individuals living the frontier life beyond the power of the central government, or a spiritual realm that might be attained somewhere beyond the present material world, some form of heaven. Such images of paradise often serve as a justification for hatred and violence. All those who are seen as obstacles on the road to paradise must be evil.

In many instances, there is a blindspot that prevents authoritarians from seeing contradictions between the paths taken to reach a utopia and the characteristics of the utopia itself. For example, in the United States extremists in the pro-life

Authoritarianism and Illusions of Control

Domains	Left-wing	Right-wing
Goals	Erradication of authoritarianism	Erradication of otherness
Assumptions	The spread of education and advances in science and technology will end prejudice and fanaticism	The world is divided between "us" and "them" I.e., "good" and "bad"
Constraints	Extreme relativist position, i.e. value free society	Fanatical utopian position

movement have been willing to kill medical personnel to "save lives." Similarly, extremist paramilitary groups are willing to blow up innocent children, women, and men, to "preserve freedom." The ultimate illusion of authoritarians may be that their movement can come to control society, that they are strong and the opposition is weak.

Concluding Comment

The liberal faith in the power of education to control ethnocentrism and authoritarianism is being severely tested at the turn of the twenty-first century. Separatist movements, from moderate nationalists in Canada, the United Kingdom, Spain, and elsewhere to radical antigovernment groups such as the Freemen in the United States, have sprung up throughout the Western world, showing that degrees of xenophobia can thrive in "advanced" industrialized countries where technology is also extremely sophisticated. Of course, part of the problem could be that education in modern industrial societies is inadequate. The liberal defense that the right kind of education *will* eradicate authoritarianism is still available. Our intention here has not been to add to what Stephen Holmes (1993) identified as the historical theme of antiliberalism, but to point out what may be a subtle but continuous weakness in the liberal armor.

Perhaps part of the solution may be to move away from an emphasis and faith in so-called value-free science and education to one where values and assumptions in science and education are explicit. This means that we must step forward in defense of identifiable values and standards, and thus necessarily move away from at least an extreme relativist position.

Critical Thinking Exercises

(1) What are the main characteristics of the authoritarian personality? Give examples of authoritarians in the modern world.
(2) The experience of Nazi Germany shows that technological progress and education will not end authoritarianism. Do you agree?

15

Controlling Conflict:
The Longest Illusion

There never was a good war, or a bad peace.

Benjamin Franklin (1706-1790)

Surely this is a universal sentiment that Franklin expresses, in a letter on 11 September, 1783. All that is noble and good in human life is associated with peace rather than war, with giving life rather than killing. True, some people do seem to prefer war to peace. For example, in William Shakespeare's *Richard III*, the play opens with Richard mourning the fact that it is a time of peace rather than war because he cannot shine in such fair, peaceful days. We recognize, however, that Richard is a monstrous villain, and his love of war is central to his villainy.

Pacifism has become a particularly powerful movement in the twentieth century. In part, this is through the influence of revolutionaries such as Karl Marx and the spread of "universal brotherhood," or "proletariate brotherhood," as a viable proposition. One is reminded here of the British World War II pacifist slogan, "A bayonet is a weapon with a worker at either end," and of the rallying cry, "Workers of the world unite."

Humanism is another powerful modern movement that has strengthened pacifism and given it a broader base. A major feature of modern humanism is the central place it gives to humankind, and the faith it assumes in human potential. Coupled with this is a refusal to rely on religion and faith in God as crutches, but if heaven and hell are to be found only on earth, then humans must take full responsibility for their destiny. Their technological capabilities allow them to choose between a great many very different possible futures, with the total destruction of the world being one possibility.

Thus the appeal of pacifism on the brink of the twenty-first century also arises because of the realization that humans have reached a point of no return. Our technological capabilities are now so advanced that the next full-scale world war could be the last. We are now capable of destroying Mother Earth and everything that lives on it, so we must think very carefully before embarking on another world war.

Why should we be optimistic about the future? Throughout our recorded history, there have constantly been wars raging in some parts of the world, and during the past century there have been two expansive world wars; why should we imagine that we can now control war and prevent catastrophe? The rationalists provide us with some justification for such optimism.

Rationalists assume that people in the social world are in an exchange situation, where each social encounter involves giving and receiving. Such an exchange viewpoint first came to the forefront in the 1950s, and is still influencing the way many researchers think about conflict, even though this influence is seldom made explicit (Taylor & Moghaddam, 1994).

War as Rational Behavior

A fundamental paradox confronts us when we review scholarly work on conflicts and conflict resolution. This paradox is all the more peculiar because the scholarly work in this domain moves across many different fields. The same paradox underlies the thinking of social scientists researching a vast array of domains - from experimental social psychology studies carried out in laboratories to theoretical political science analyses, from gaming research conducted on computers to field research carried out in real-life settings, from "war game" simulations to participant observation studies in actual conflict situations. Underlying the vast majority of this research is the assumption that people behave rationally and that the best account of conflict is provided by a rational person (Fisher, 1989).

People are assumed to be involved in give and take and to be continually keeping accounts of their profits and losses. The objective of such behavior is assumed to be that people want to maximize their profits. Conflict arises when parties in an interaction see their incompatible interests as more important (for profit making) than their compatible ones: when, for example, two nations think they can gain control of oil fields in a region, and what they may gain by fighting to gain control is more than what they could gain by cooperating with one another. An example from the business world would be, when two pharmaceutical companies believe they have more to gain by competing to develop a new drug independent of one another than by joining forces and cooperating on the project but having to share profits at a later stage. This has gone so far in the pharmaceutical industry that there have now been well over 100 so-called me-too drugs developed for hypertension.

Thus, the rational view of conflict sees the parties as being in a marketplace and acting rather like accounting machines that rationally compute estimates of profits and losses and select the most profitable alternatives. This viewpoint is all the more paradoxical because it assumes that the "marketplace" is rational. That is, in order for the marketplace model to be valid, behavior in the marketplace has to be rational. This is, of course, a far too simplistic assumption. One of the illusions underlying economic theory is the rational model of humankind. It is all too easy to see how behavior on the stock market and in business generally can be depicted as irrational rather than rational.

The Prisoner's Dilemma Game: The Rationalist Approach Encapsulated

The rationalist approach to conflict is encapsulated wonderfully in the prisoner's dilemma game (PDG). This is a fairly simple game with many different variations; its popularity is shown by the thousands of studies published using the PDG procedure.

The PDG owes its name to an imaginary scenario involving two criminals who have been captured and are being cross-examined by the police. The prisoners are kept in separate cells, and the dilemma arises because each prisoner must chance a guess about what the other is going to do. Will the other cooperate with the police and tell them everything? Will the other keep quite? If they both keep silent and refuse to inform the police about the other's role in the crime, then they both get off with a light sentence. If, however, only one of them refuses to talk and the other "snitches," then the one who has not cooperated will get a very long prison sentence and the one who has talked will walk away free. If they both talk, they get a medium sentence, longer than they would if they both kept silent.

It is easy to see how this simple game was extended to the domain of international conflict. Countries or military blocks can take the place of the prisoners. Two rival countries have to guess what the other is going to do: for example, will the enemy maintain, increase, or decrease its level of military spending? If the enemy increases military spending and we do not, then the enemy could overpower us. If we increase, and the enemy decreases, we might overpower them, but we could also ruin our economy and collapse financially (after all, the collapse of the USSR was ultimately economic).

Business rivals often face the same dilemma. Company X could collaborate with a rival by jointly investing in the development of a new product; however, joint investment would not bring the highest level of profits. If company X goes it alone, the investment might not prove to be fruitful and might result in financial ruin. On the other hand, if company X neglects this new product opportunity altogether, its rival may go it alone, reap all the rewards, and dominate the market in the future.

A key assumption in the PDG is that all decision makers have to work in an

information vacuum. Thus, in the classic PDG scenario each prisoner sits alone in the cell pondering this dilemma, deliberating what to do in order to arrive at the best possible outcome for *himself*, which brings us to another key feature of the rational model. It assumes that people are selfish and will try to maximize their own profits.

The rationalist theorists have even tried to explain seemingly altruistic acts such as sacrificing oneself for one's group as being self-serving in important respects. Such sacrifices occur among humans (as in dying for one's country), but they also occur among animals. For example, it is not unusual among small birds for one of them to give a warning call when a falcon or some other predator bird arrives on the scene. By giving the warning signal, a bird will reveal its own location to the predator and be more likely to become the predator's next meal. If organisms are selfish, why should they act in such a (seemingly) heroic way?

Rationalism and Sociobiology

One answer has been provided by sociobiology, which involves the application of biological principles to social behavior, among human and nonhuman groups (e.g., Buss, 1994). According to the sociobiological thesis, particularly as elaborated in *The Selfish Gene* and other writings by Dawkins (1976), organisms will sacrifice themselves only if by doing so they improve the chances of survival of their gene pool. The key theme in evolution, then, is competition between genes, rather than individuals. In a sense, humans and animals are simply convenient vehicles for genes, they serve a useful purpose because they act as gene carriers. It is the survival of genes that is of primary importance, rather than the carriers. From this viewpoint, then, what looks like heroism and a sacrifice on the part of an individual is actually a strategy for serving the selfish interests of the gene pool.

This selfish gene perspective serves as the basis for the rational account of conflict, at both interindividual and intergroup levels. Sociobiologists have amassed evidence to support the thesis that people will harm others who are genetically dissimilar to themselves. In their comprehensive work entitled *Homicide*, Daly and Wilson (1988) attempted to substantiate their thesis that the victims of homicide are in general genetically dissimilar to the perpetrators. For example, adopted children and stepchildren are far more likely to be victims in domestic violence than are natural children. One explanation is that parents look after their own offspring much better than they do genetically dissimilar children. Similarly, married couples, who are never closely related, are more likely to kill one another than they are to kill their own offspring.

Van den Berghe (1987) has extended this line of argument to show that in collective conflict, the target of attack is generally a genetically dissimilar outgroup. He pointed out that in North America there is a long history of discrimination against African-Americans and other ethnic minorities. His main point is that such minorities are the victims of discrimination because they are identified as being genetically dissimilar from the white majority group. Of course, it is not just in the North American context that this argument sounds plausible; North Africans in France, Turks in Germany, and South Asians in England are among the many other examples that could be plausibly cited.

A Rational Spiral toward Destructive Conflict

The rationalist account of conflict finds its most convincing voice in Morton Deutsch (1993), who is also an excellent representative for the American liberal tradition on the issue of conflict. Central to this tradition is an optimistic conviction that humans actually desire peace and want to avoid war.

Since peace is desired and war is abhorred, then how is it that wars occur? The answer, it seems, is dramatically simple: war occurs by mistake. The parties in a conflict do not intend to make war, but they misunderstand one another, make wrong assumptions about what the other is thinking and intending to do, and then slide down a spiral of destructive conflict. At each step during this process, they see the other as a threat and then proceed to interpret as threatening whatever the other is doing.

Given this assessment of the situation, the solution to conflict is obvious. Conflict resolution is achieved when we bring an end to misunderstandings and misperceptions. Once the parties in a conflict realize what the other is really thinking and wanting, which is (presumably) to live in peace and to enjoy a higher standard of living, then they will be able to put aside their own fears and participate in a peaceful relationship.

Superordinate Goals

The supreme contribution of the rationalist approach has been to propose superordinate goals as the solution to conflict situations. These are goals that all parties in a conflict situation want to achieve, but that can only be achieved if all parties combine forces and cooperate. For example, environmental protection can be considered a superordinate goal because it is presumably in the interests of all humankind to save Planet Earth. However, in order to achieve this goal and solve problems such as ozone depletion, all the major nations must cooperate.

The major challenge becomes that of helping everyone to recognize, to actually see, such superordinate goals. It is assumed that once they achieve such a recognition, then they will do what is best for their own interests. Note that the concept of superordinate goals still assumes that people are basically self-centered. When they fail to behave in a way that best serves their own interests, it is not because they are unselfish, but rather because they have not had access to the information that would allow them to maximize their own personal profits.

Concluding Comment

The rationalist model of conflict assumes people are self-centered and try to maximize their own "profits." They do this through a step-by-step analysis of their interactions with others, that leads to an estimate of how much they put in and how much they get out of each episode.

A curious relationship exists between the frequency of national, regional, and world wars and the number of "peace institutes" thriving around the world. As humankind suffers through more wars, more and more "peace institutes" and peace studies programs mushroom into existence. Another curious aspect of this situation is that despite all evidence to the contrary, the economic exchange model of conflict continues to dominate peace studies.

Critical Thinking Exercises

(1) What is the prisoners dilemma game and in what ways does it represent the rationalist approach to conflict?
(2) We are in control of conflict, but we have not wanted to end it badly enough. Do you agree?

16

The Paradox of Technology and Conflict Control

"But we have to put more money into the military."
"Of course we do."
"Speak softly, but carry a big stick! Never forget that."
"Of course not."
"As long as we have arms superiority, we have peace."
"That's for sure."

The two Englishmen having this conversation were waiting to board flights at London's Heathrow Airport, but they could have been American, or Russian, or Chinese, or from just about anywhere else on earth. The sentiment that military might will allow us to control intergroup relationships and secure peace is pervasive in many societies. It is a sentiment worth examining in more detail, particularly because the real paradox of military weapons is that they have put humans out of control, rather than in control.

Modern Weapons and Aggression

There is little doubt that in terms of sheer technical innovation and creativity, experts have achieved amazing feats in the realm of weapons. Research expertise has created the opportunity for us to kill millions of people on the other side of the globe, and even to blow up the entire world. The development of Smart Weapons shows the way for the future, with weapons becoming increasingly capable of "intelligently" tracking and hunting down their targets, even though such targets may lie hidden or camouflaged for prolonged periods (although some people will protest the idea of anything military being described as intelligent). These are not small achievements when viewed strictly from a technical standpoint.

The ability to kill others from a distance is a technological innovation that, according to Nobel prize winner Konrad Lorenz (1966), sidesteps the inhibitory mechanisms that had come in place through evolution to help prevent within-species killing among humans. Lorenz's brilliant book *On Aggression* explains this thesis: At an early stage of evolution, when they had not yet developed weapons, humans had effective ways of avoiding killing each other. These inhibitory mechanisms had taken a very long time to evolve, but they were compatible with the killing powers of weaponless humans.

The Role of Inhibitory Mechanisms

The role of inhibitory mechanisms can be clarified by considering other species. Within-species fighting among animals has the function of selecting which male will have access to females, and thus which individuals will have the opportunity to pass on their genes to the next generation. Fighting between two male wolves, or two stallions, or two male lions, to cite a few examples, will very seldom result in the death of one of the combatants. When death does occur, it is usually an accident. (One of us witnessed two stags who had starved to death after their antlers were locked during fighting, so neither could escape.) In the vast majority of fights between two males of the same species, the conflict ends when the loser signals defeat and is chased out of the arena.

Gorillas provide an interesting example of this thesis. Once a loser among two fighting gorillas signals defeat, the winner does not then chase the loser with an intent to kill. The winner only chases the loser out of his territory, to ensure the loser does not have access to the females in his harem. The signals that the defeated gorilla gives to indicate his estimation of the situation are read by the winner, and this reading leads to inhibition of aggression. An important point is that the inhibitory mechanisms of an animal like the gorilla match its primitive aggressive capabilities. If a gorilla could operate a bazooka, then there would be a mismatch between its capabilities and the inhibitory mechanisms at work among gorillas.

To better understand what Lorenz meant by inhibitory mechanisms matching primitive killing capabilities, just imagine trying to kill another person with your bare hands. The other person could take a variety of actions to try to stop you - running away, calling for help, pleading with you. Even if you manage to corner the other person alone, you would have to touch, smell, see, in some way be in human contact with the person you are trying to kill. This would make killing the other person much more difficult.

Inhibitory Mechanisms and Modern Weapons

If you can fire an arrow from several hundred meters away, or a rifle from several miles away, or a missile from hundreds or thousands of miles away, then killing becomes much easier. If all we see of an enemy is a light that appears on a radar screen and then disappears after the bomb has been dropped or the missile launched, then human contact is minimized and the evolutionary inhibitory mechanisms designed to prevent within species killing is sidestepped.

This relationship between target distance and the tendency of people to act aggressively was demonstrated by Stanley Milgram in what is perhaps the most controversial social psychology experiment in history. Milgram screened a normal sample of people to play the role of teachers in his study. Their task was to teach word associations to other subjects (actually confederates of Milgram) who acted as learners. Each time the learner made a mistake, the teacher was supposed to administer an increasingly higher level of electric shock as punishment. This whole episode was overlooked by an authority figure, a scientist in a white lab coat. Neither experts nor laypeople had predicted the results of this study. American studies show that something like two-thirds of the subjects were prepared to administer lethal levels of electric shock to the learner (even higher levels of obedience were reported in studies in some countries outside the United States). Most relevant to our discussion is the finding that the greater the distance between the teacher and the learner/victim, the greater the likelihood of shock being administered.

For example, the likelihood of electric shock being administered increased when the teacher was situated in another room and could shock the learner/victim without witnessing the reactions and pleas for the shocks to stop.

Modern Weapons and Decreasing Control

According to Lorenz's thesis, then, our increased capacity to create more powerful weapons has actually led to a situation where we have less control over our own aggressive behavior. The consequence is that at both the interpersonal and intergroup levels, violence has dramatically increased. During the twentieth century we have seen the outcome of this lack of control. We have outdone ourselves as a species in the total number of our own kind that we have managed to kill. Each war has brought new records. Wold War I and World War II have been the highlights, but many regional conflicts have also involved enormous numbers of casualties.

At the interpersonal level, also, modern technology has given us increased capabilities, and decreased control. This is exemplified by the situation that exists in the inner cities of the most powerful and technologically advanced nation in the world, the United States. The major U.S. urban centers house research centers of tremendous technological capabilities, feeding directly or indirectly into arms production, MIT in Boston, NASA in Washington, CALTECH in California, but ironically, it is not safe to walk around at night (or in some cases during the daytime!) in some of these urban centers. The availability of firearms means that those committed to violent crime are able to kill their victims using the latest technology. The rapid-firing automatic weapons available on the streets of

Washington, D.C., would match or beat equivalent light weapons found in the most advanced professional armies.

Weapons, Control, and International Conflict

The case of how international conflict has been dealt with demonstrates in a dramatic manner the persistence of a rigid notion of control, one that is commonly associated with illusions. During the twentieth century there has not been a time when wars have not been raging in some part of the world. Modern weapons have meant that what might have previously been a low-casualty conflict is now more likely to involve high casualties. Also, the most powerful and rich nations are able to put advanced weapons in the hands of strategically placed rebels in other countries, and such weapons can allow even small bands of rebels to make a significant mark on local events, by harassing and killing large numbers of people.

Side by side with this highly inflammable world situation is a set of activities designed to control conflict, and often serving to strengthen the illusion that all is well. One example of such activities comes under the umbrella of what might loosely be termed U.N. peace efforts. Our point here is not that the U.N. system is totally useless, but that the function it actually serves is often very different from the espoused peace-keeping one. If we want an illustrative example of this point, we need not look very far. The Bosnian situation serves this purpose well enough. Since the beginning of ethnic conflict in the former Yugoslavia, the United Nations has proved to be powerless to stop the fighting in Bosnia, and critics do not seem to have a solution either. The most constructive suggestion made by critics (such as leaders of the Republican party in the United States) of the present U.N. policy is that the arms embargo should be lifted, so that the weaker side can get better armed. Presumably, increasing people's capabilities to kill will lead to peace.

The United Nations is perhaps the most visible symbol of peace-keeping efforts, but there are thousands of other institutions and hundreds of thousands of experts around the world involved in peace keeping. Their activities result in thousands of meetings, seminars, and conferences each year and the publication of mountains of books, journals, and other materials. One of the consequences of these varied activities is a sense of control. Something *is* being done about violence, so we must have some control over the situation.

Obviously, we are not claiming that peace conferences are not useful and that talks are not effective in bringing fighting parties closer together. However, it is important to keep in mind that often peace talks merely serve a psychological function of allowing people to assume they are doing something to end conflict. Peace, when it arrives, is often the consequence of circumstances and an option that is taken when no other alternative exists (for example, did the Germans or Japanese really have any option other than to agree to peace terms at the end of

World War I and World War II?).

Concluding Comment

The view that advances in military technology lead to peace is naive because it only allows for peace on the terms and conditions of those nations who have the advanced technology. Sooner or later, other nations catch up in military power and challenge the old order, either at the negotiation table or on the battlefield, or both. Modern weapons mean that humans are "out of control" of the evolutionary-developed inhibitory mechanisms designed to prevent same-species killing. One way to improve our chances of survival is to create conditions in which those mechanisms are once again effective.

Critical Thinking Exercises

(1) What does Lorenz mean by inhibitory mechanisms?
(2) In what ways have modern weapons put humans outside the control of inhibitory mechanisms?

17

Control of the Ethereal: Cultural and Values

Turning and turning in the widening gyre
The falcon cannot hear the falconer;
Things fall apart; the centre cannot hold;
Mere anarchy is loosed upon the world,
The blood-dimmed tide is loosed, and everywhere
The ceremony of innocence is drowned;
The best lack all conviction, while the worst
are full of passionate intensity.
Surely some revelation is at hand;
Surely the Second Coming is at hand.

William Butler Yeats, *The Second Coming*

Yeats seems to have expressed what many people feel about the world as they view it on the brink of the twenty-first century. The central tenets of traditional Western culture seem to be falling apart. These changes are particularly lamented by conservatives because they involve a loss of respect for authority, the demise of family values, the death of traditional religion and community, and a feeling that anything goes in the newly emerging youth cultures.

Most generally, the postmodern age has brought with it a relativistic viewpoint, whereby the universal validity of traditional values is challenged. As Allan Bloom (1987) pointed out when discussing the characteristics of modern students in his critical text *The Closing of the American Mind*, "There is one thing a professor can be absolutely certain of: almost every student entering the university believes, or says he believes, that truth is relative" (p. 25).

The superiority of one value system over others is rejected by relativism because each value system is seen to be valid only within the cultural context in which it has evolved. For example, consider the issue of how the crime of bank robbery might be punished in different societies. In a Western society, the thief would typically be sentenced to prison. In a society where traditional Islamic laws are adhered to, the thief might have one hand cut off. A relativist perspective leads us to ask, who is to say that putting a man in jail for fifteen years, where he could face isolation, persecution, rape, and other cruelties, is more humane than chopping off one of his hands?

In the context of Western societies, it is no longer just taken for granted that the traditional white male Christian view of the world is the correct one because minorities also hold value systems that "have a right" to be heard in the new cultural climate. This leads to the offering of new university courses with titles like, Dead White Male Writers, which invite students to evaluate classics such as *Hamlet* from an alternative viewpoint.

The culture wars that have raged in North America, Europe, and elsewhere are all the more fierce because they have become moral crusades. Contemporary students see the relativity of truth as a moral postulate rather than a theoretical insight, and they believe relativism to be necessary for open-mindedness (Bloom, 1987). If you believe there is a universally correct standard on a certain issue, then presumably you are *not* going to tolerate my alternative viewpoint. It seems, then, that only relativists can give my alternative viewpoint a fair hearing.

Both supporters of a universalist view and those of a relativist perspective are under the influence of certain illusions about controlling culture. Historically, by far the most influential among these illusions have been the ones held by the universalists because they have been the dominant group. It has only been since the late 1960s that the position of the universalists has been seriously challenged.

Universalism and Illusions of Controlling Culture

In response to the question, What kind of a society should we strive to achieve? the universalists have argued that it must be a culturally homogeneous one. In response to the question, What should be the basis for the normative system we choose for society? they have proposed that natural laws should serve this purpose, because these are the laws that they see as inherent in human nature.

Nowhere is the universalist position more starkly portrayed than in the United States, and more specifically in the U.S. policy of assimilation, or the melting pot. From its inception, the United States has been known as a land of immigrants, as a magnet for people from many different religious, linguistic, ethnic, and national backgrounds. From the beginning of U.S. history, the main policy adopted for managing cultural diversity has been assimilation. That is, immigrants have been expected to change themselves through assimilation, so that despite the cultural and linguistic diversity of new arrivals, the outcome remains a homogeneous society (see Moghaddam & Solliday, 1991).

Different Styles of Assimilation

Assimilation can take place in a number of different ways. A first and perhaps the simplest model is "minority group assimilation," which involves only the minority group members changing, to become more like the majority group. This is a unidirectional change, so that minorities become absorbed into the mainstream. This involves, for example, the transformation of Greek, Polish, Russian, and other groups of immigrants to the United States, so that after a time they become Americans and are in all important respects indistinguishable from the American mainstream.

Minority group assimilation assumes that there is a fairly stable and easily identifiable American mainstream. Given the regionalism of the United States, it is inevitable that such a mainstream can have only very broad and hazy characteristics if it is to be effective nationally. For example, even if one takes the mainstream standard to be a white Anglo-Saxon Protestant (WASP) male, there would be disagreement about the more detailed characteristics of this standard in the North and South, as well as in the eastern, central, and western parts of the United States. The Southern gentleman and the New England gentleman would have much to quarrel about when it comes to ideals and standards, to mention just one instance of diversity in the mainstream.

Despite being unrealistic in its assumptions about the existence of a nationally accepted ideal, minority group assimilation has given the majority group in America at least a mechanism for maintaining their higher status. Although they cannot define precisely what is the mainstream standard to which immigrants should try to live up to, they can still use this illusive ideal to at least distance themselves, as well as to justify their higher status. Perhaps this ideal is all the more useful for such a purpose because it is so illusive. If outsiders cannot pinpoint it, then it is all the more difficult to attain.

In practice, it is not minority group assimilation but melting-pot assimilation that has been most widespread. This latter involves a bi-directional process, whereby all minority and majority groups give and take, influence one another, and evolve culturally.

Melting-pot assimilation has been the inevitable outcome of certain ecological conditions in the United States, such as the pressure cooker conditions immigrants experienced in major cities like New York, as well as in the frontier during the great Western expansion. Thrown together in harsh conditions, immigrants from different religious, linguistic, and national backgrounds had to mingle and cooperate in order to improve their chances of survival. Even if they were not moved by a love of one another or a humanitarian fervor, the practical needs of day-to-day survival forced immigrants to close ranks so as to survive hostile conditions.

Assimilation in the "Old World"

We are accustomed to think about the United States as a land of immigrants and to conceptualize culture change in the New World, in contrast to which the Old World seems stable. The stability of the Old World is to a large extent illusory since there, also, melting-pot assimilation is taking place. For example, since World War II the mainstream culture in England, France, and Germany has been transformed through many different influences, including the arrival of millions of immigrants from vastly different cultural backgrounds; some obvious examples being South Asians to England, North Africans to France, Turks to Germany.

Although each of these groups of new arrivals to the European scene has a different history and came to Europe for reasons that are to some extent unique, they have one very important thing in common: they all impact on the cultural life of the host European society. Just as North Africans have changed the cultural scene of France, South Asians have influenced cultural life in England. Of course, during this process the minorities have themselves been transformed culturally.

Cultural Assimilation in the European Community

In the context of recent European events, the universalist position is better reflected in the move toward establishing a "European community" than by the case of minority group immigrants in European societies. The assumption has been that Europe would become unified not only economically and politically but also culturally. Presumably, the populations of EEC member states would become culturally similar and would identify more strongly with the European community, and less with their own particular national groupings.

A Challenge to Universalist-Assimilationist Assumptions

Assumptions that there would emerge a homogeneous American culture in conformity with WASP or any other mainstream ideals have been severely tested, if not invalidated outright, by events during the latter part of the twentieth century. The "ethnic revival" has been a worldwide movement, but its strength and vitality has been particularly intense in the United States. Nourished by collective movements such as black power, womens liberation, and gay rights, hundreds of different ethnic, linguistic, and cultural minority movements have emerged in the United States. What these minority movements have in common is an insistence that their culture, their way of doing things, is as valuable as any other, and that they have the right to preserve and celebrate cultural differences.

In many cases such minority ethnic movements have enjoyed an economic base. For example, the strength of Hispanic linguistic and cultural distinctiveness in the United States arises in large part from what have been termed "ethnic economic enclaves" monopolized by Hispanics in cities such as Miami. Hispanics can maintain their language and their distinctiveness in Miami because they control businesses, and this enables them to provide and to take away jobs.

The ethnic revival, together with various alternative movements, such as the green movement, has given visibility to a greater number of groups with which individuals can identify. For example, a Cuban immigrant has the possibility of identifying with the Cuban group, with subgroups within the Cuban community (e.g., gay Cubans, Republican Cubans, etc.) or with the larger "American" society. In response to the question, Which is your most important group membership? an African-American can respond, "I am first a Black," or ". . . a feminist," or " . . . an American," or ". . . a physician," or ". . . a lawyer." The American dream is still a rags-to-riches story, but the end of the rainbow no longer means becoming a good WASP.

The illusion of control among universalists has been that they could shape cultural development and control the evolution of society, so that newly arrived immigrants would transform themselves and conform to the majority group model of the "American ideal." Even now, when the fallacy of this illusion has been exposed by practical experience, some die-hard universalists are fighting back to try to reestablish uniformity to a majority model of what it is to be an American. This is reflected, for example, in the so-called English only movement that, among other things, seeks to establish English as the official language of the United States.

Assimilationist Illusions and the European Community

The assumption that the European community would become culturally integrated has proved to be illusory, so far at least. This lack of cultural integration is influencing political decision making. For example, the reactions of the EEC member states to events during the 1990s in Yugoslavia, Russia, and other former Communist Bloc countries are influenced more by regional and national values and interests than they are by a "common European outlook." Because regionalism and nationalism still dictate EEC policy, there has yet to emerge a "European" outlook on many sensitive issues. Consequently, if the United States does not take the lead in dealing with a crisis in a region such as Yugoslavia, then it is almost certain that the EEC will remain ineffective.

Multiculturalism and Illusions of Cultural Freedom

During the last few decades of the twentieth century, multiculturalism has replaced assimilation as the dominant strategy for managing cultural diversity in the United States, as well as in other regions of the world. The term "multiculturalism" is used rather loosely to refer to ethnic pluralism and to a "celebration of differences." Implicit in this loose definition is the idea of ethnic pride, as well as minority rights.

In some societies, such as Canada and Australia, multiculturalism has taken on more specific meanings. This is partly because in order to officially base government policy on multiculturalism, this rather vague term has had to be interpreted more precisely. Such official policies involve government support for the retention and sharing of heritage cultures and languages.

Multiculturalism seems to make available to people a much larger variety of cultural groups with which they can freely choose to identify. Thus, in the United States the term "multiculturalism" is often equated with liberation and cultural freedom. Implicit in this is the idea of people enjoying greater freedom to choose their own way.

The availability of many different groups with which one may identify should not lead us to assume that Americans are nonconformists. Tocqueville (1845) pointed out long ago in *Democracy in America* that although Americans talk a great deal about independence of mind and freedom of thought, there is considerable uniformity of thought in U.S. society. This situation has not changed much in modern times, first because there is remarkable conformity within the various different groups with which Americans identify, and second because these groups are mostly symbolically rather than actually different.

When they are given a choice between upper, middle, and lower class, over 90 percent of Americans identify themselves as middle class. This perceived uniformity of social classes allows for all kinds of symbolic differences to become important in American society.

For example, consider the case of one of the most important ethnic movements in recent history, the Black Power movement, which began in the 1960s in the United States. Despite all the talk of "cultural differences," the unique marker of African Americans in the United States has been their phenotypic characteristics, rather than their cultural characteristics. It is the symbolic difference of skin color that serves as the basis for both discrimination against blacks and the mobilization of their group. Middle-class blacks are more similar to middle-class whites than they are to working-class blacks in terms of lifestyle; black doctors and lawyers are much more similar to white doctors and lawyers in their lifestyle than they are to working-class Blacks. However, these actual group similarities and differences prove not to be as important as the symbolic criterion of skin color when it comes to ethnic identification and collective action.

The Relation Between Free Market Conditions and Differentiation

The policies of assimilation and multiculturalism assume different relationships between free market conditions and differentiation in social development. Assimilation policy assumes that cultural homogeneity will create "level conditions" to act as a platform for meritocracy. That is, through taking on the majority culture and language, minority children will have the same chances as children from mainstream families to succeed in open competition. In this way, cultural homogeneity will allow whoever has most merit to rise to the top.

Open competition will in turn lead to social differentiation. Individuals and groups will diverge and proceed along different uninhabited paths in order to occupy vacant spaces and have access to greater resources. In most instances, "resources" will have a bearing on social status.

A policy of multiculturalism assumes that freedom to choose one's own path in cultural development will lead to cultural diversity. That is, people will choose to belong to culturally diverse, differentiated groups. Thus, differentiation is a direct outcome of cultural freedom.

Concluding Comment

The major policies for managing cultural diversity have assumed that cultural evolution can be controlled. On the one hand, assimilationists thought that they could mold a homogeneous society; on the other hand, multiculturalists believed that they could develop a cultural mosaic. In practice, cultural development seems to proceed in complex ways, influenced by many economic, political, social, technological, and other factors, none of which are effectively controlled by people inside or outside government. In effect, the level of control over cultural life has been exaggerated.

Critical Thinking Exercises

(1) What are the main differences between assimilation and multiculturalism?
(2) Assimilation and multicultualism both assume we have control over cultural development. Explain.

18

Motivation and Control of Cultural Development

If aliens had landed in the United States during the legal trial of O. J. Simpson, the famous African American football star accused of murdering his former wife and a friend, they might have concluded that there two types of Americans: Pro-O. J. and anti-O. J. The former would have been predominantly black, the latter predominantly white. Despite this collective, group-based response to the O. J. Simpson affair, American analysts continue to discuss this issue as if it involved only individual judgments.

The ethos of individualism leads Americans to give reductionist explanations of behavior. That is, to explain behavior through reference to intrapersonal processes, rather than to the characteristics of social life and normative systems.

In answer to the question, "Why does Samantha think O. J. Simpson should have been convicted?" the response is, "Because she has thought it through and come to this conclusion," rather than, "Because she is white," or "Because Samantha is a woman." The issue of motivation, why people behave as they do, is reduced to the personal level.

Reductionist accounts of motivation underlie even the most progressive theories of intergroup relations (Taylor & Moghaddam, 1994), as well as the major accounts of multiculturalism (Moghaddam, 1993). The traditional view of motivation matches the "self-contained individualism" of American dominated modern psychology, whereby the destinies of individuals are viewed as causally determined by factors inside persons (Hofstede, 1980; Moghaddam, 1998). The American dream propagates the view that the social system is open, and that the movement of individuals up and down the status hierarchy is completely dependent on personal characteristics, chiefly motivation. The American motto seems to be, "If you really want it, you can get it," implying that those who do not make progress in the system only have themselves (or, more precisely, their motivation) to blame. The intrapersonal motivation theory also embodies a causal account of behavior paradoxically in tension with the personal attribution of responsibility found in an individualistic culture.

In addition to explaining the social status of individuals in terms of personal characteristics ("He is motivated!" "She is a go-getter!"), this reductionist approach explains intergroup relations through reference to intrapersonal characteristics. For example, discrimination against out-group members is described as being caused by personality characteristics of individuals, such as levels of self-esteem or a broader array of features under headings such as an "authoritarian personality" type (Adorno, Frenkel-Brunswik, Levisnon, & Sanford, 1950). Similarly, the major models of multiculturalism rest on assumptions about intra-personal psychological functioning (Moghaddam, 1992, 1993; Moghaddam & Solliday, 1991).

An alternative view is to adopt a more *social* explanation of intergroup relations, an explanation that incorporates patterns of social life and the normative systems that govern social relationships (see Moghaddam & Harré, 1995, for a review of traditional and alternative approaches). From this alternative viewpoint, human behavior is not "caused" by motivation inside individuals, but is patterned along social norms and structured by reference to extra-personally located rules available to individuals. Motivation itself is viewed as embedded in normative systems, rather than in the private psyche of individual persons. Such normative systems consist of norms, general prescriptions for socially appropriate behavior, and rules, maxims describing correct behavior for individuals in interdependent role-relations (e.g., parent-child, professor-student, doctor-patient).

In the first part of the chapter we discuss attempts by Tajfel (1978), considered by many to be the father of European social psychology, to move beyond reductionist accounts of intergroup relations. We argue that even social identity theory (Tajfel & Turner, 1979), the most influential modern intergroup theory, remains reductionist because it interprets intergroup bias as arising from motivational states internal to individuals. In the second part, we critically assess the assumed role of motivation in policies for managing cultural diversity, including multiculturalism policy.

Intergroup Discrimination on a Trivial Basis

> It is computed, that eleven thousand persons have, at several times, suffered death, rather than submit to break their eggs at the smaller end. Many hundred large volumes have been published upon this controversy: but the books of the Big-Endians have been long forbidden, and the whole party rendered incapable by law of holding employment...a bloody war hath been carried on between the two empires (Little-Endians and Big-Endians) for six and thirty moons.

Jonathan Swift, *Lilliput* (1960, pp.39-40)

It is during his voyage to Lilliput that Gulliver, Jonathan Swift's timeless character, receives this account of the war between those who persist in breaking eggs at the little end and their bitter enemies, those who insist that eggs must only be broken at the big end. Swift's satirical insights reveal that even what seem to be trivial differences between groups can act as a basis for intergroup conflicts. Two and a half centuries later psychologists provided empirical demonstrations of this very same insight, showing how even minimal differences between categories of people can lead to intergroup discrimination (Tajfel, 1982).

The minimal group studies conducted by Tajfel and his associates have been discussed extensively, and have generated a robust literature (see Taylor & Moghaddam, 1994, ch. 4). The minimal group paradigm involves two stages. First, participants are divided into two groups on the basis of a criterion generally judged to be trivial in the context of life outside the laboratory (e.g., social categorization is on the basis of a dot-estimation task, or picture preferences, or a toss of a coin). Research participants have no contact with, or knowledge about, in-group and out-group members, other than their category memberships. In a second stage, participants have an opportunity to allocate points to in-group and out-group members.

The often replicated finding is that participants in the minimal group paradigm allocate more points to the in-group than to the out-group. Tajfel and his associates have interpreted this bias as arising from a need participants have to achieve a positive and distinct social identity, defined as "that part of an individual's self-concept which derives from his knowledge of his membership in a social group (or groups) together with the value and emotional significance attached to that membership" (Tajfel, 1978, p. 63). Interestingly, social identity theory was developed in an attempt to move away from the reductionism of U.S. dominated mainstream social psychology. However, by focusing on the individual as the source of motivation leading to intergroup biases, it seems to us that Tajfel and his associates have also followed a reductionist line of argument.

Rather than pointing to apparently stable motivational states of individuals, we prefer to seek explanations in the normative system. Participants in the minimal group paradigm ask themselves (as do all participants in laboratory experiments, see Moghaddam & Harré, 1992), "What is the correct way for me to behave in this context? How should I behave in order to be seen as doing the right thing?" Tajfel's research participants were drawn from a culture in which random selection of teams for sporting contests was a common practice. The idea that people from non-Western cultures may behave differently in the minimal group paradigm receives support from a study involving European, Samoan, and Maori participants, in which the latter two samples showed less in-group favoritism than the first sample (Wetherell, 1982).

In a situation where there is only one clue to guide social action, the categorization of the social world into in-group and out-group members, the participants use this clue to guide their actions. Experimental evidence suggests

that irrespective of whether the basis for categorization is trivial or important in the world outside the laboratory, when it is the only guide for action in the experimental situation then it is ascribed significance and meaning by participants so that their own actions can become meaningful (Taylor & Moghaddam, 1994, pp. 76-77). Thus, what is taken to be a "motivation" for showing bias is actually a norm extracted from the social world; it is not something inherent and stable in individuals.

Motivation and Policies for Managing Cultural Diversity

In this second part of the chapter, we argue that a reductionist view of motivation also pervades policies for managing cultural diversity. It is assumed that intra-personal motivation causally determines relations between cultural groups, as well as determining the success or failure of particular policies for managing cultural diversity. The major policies available for managing cultural diversity range from complete assimilation, where minority groups abandon their heritage cultures and "melt into" the majority culture, and total multiculturalism, whereby differences between groups are maintained, or even accentuated, and heritage cultures of different groups are given equal importance and kept alive. Initial steps have been taken to assess the psychological underpinnings of these alternative policies (Lambert & Taylor, 1990; Moghaddam, 1993), but more attention needs to be given to the overriding assumption that prejudice and discrimination against others is motivated by a lack of confidence in one's own identity (for a related discussion, see Harre, 1984, ch. 10).

There is a pervasive belief that motivations in the domain of intergroup relations can be shaped through influencing feelings of security. This belief is so pervasive (for examples, see Hogg & Abrams, 1990; Lambert, Mermegis, & Taylor, 1986) that it is found among the members of opposing camps in the ongoing and often heated debates concerning minority-majority relations and multiculturalism. Let us begin by highlighting this belief among supporters of multiculturalism.

In the Pro-Multiculturalism Camp

We shall focus mainly on Canada's influential multiculturalism policy, Canada being the first officially multicultural nation in the world (Lambert & Taylor, 1990). At the heart of Canada's multiculturalism policy is the so-called multiculturalism hypothesis, which proposes a direct relationship between feelings of security and intergroup behavior (Taylor, 1991). The hypothesis is central to the historic statement on multiculturalism policy by the prime minister of Canada, Pierre Elliot Trudeau, in the House of Commons, October 8, 1971:

> A policy of multiculturalism within a bilingual framework commends
> itself to the government as the most suitable means of assuring the

cultural freedom of Canadians. Such a policy should help to break down discriminatory attitudes and cultural jealousies, national unity, if it is to mean anything in the deeply personal sense, must be founded on confidence in one's own individual identity; out of this can grow respect for that of others and a willingness to share ideas, attitudes, and assumptions. A vigorous policy of multiculturalism will help create this initial confidence. It can form the base of a society which is based on fair play for all.

Trudeau was speaking in a language that is very familiar to psychologists. The central assumption that out of a "confidence in one's own identity" can "grow respect for that of others" could have come from a model of intergroup relations developed by psychologists. Indeed, this assumption was tested by psychologists, and shown to be wanting in some ways (Taylor & Moghaddam, 1994).

Comparing Swiss "Magic Formula" with the "Melting-Pot"

It is instructive to also consider a form of multiculturalism represented by culturally diverse societies organized as federations. The quintessential example of this is Switzerland, where "conflict-solution . . . relies on power sharing rather than competition for power" (Linder, 1994, p. 31). This "magic formula" hypothesis (inspired by *Zauberformel* of the Swiss Federal Council) proposes that society should be organized as a cultural mosaic, with representation being based on proportionality rather than majority takes all. In practice, this means that minorities will be represented in key public sector positions, even though they did not receive the majority of the votes (if the position is that of an elected representative) and even though they may not be the most technically capable candidates (if it is a position requiring technical expertise). In the Swiss context, the magic formula requires that in some domains only proposals that receive support from a double majority, a majority of the population and a majority of cantons (geographical units), are adopted. This means that the smaller cantons can vote to prevent the ratification of a proposal, even if it has been endorsed by the majority of the Swiss population. Implicit in this magic formula is the assumption that, just as in Canadian multiculturalism, acceptance of others is motivated by feelings of confidence in one's own group position.

Something akin to a "melting-pot" hypothesis has become influential among supporters of assimilationism, historically dominant in the United States and now also prominent as a policy option in the United Kingdom and some other European societies (Moghaddam, 1993). This hypothesis also has as its starting point an assumed relationship between feelings of security and intergroup behavior. Three assumptions are implicit in this hypothesis. First, only a majority group that is secure in its own identity can be accepting toward minority groups (such "acceptance" usually implies allowing individual "newcomers" the opportunity to join mainstream society through a long-term process of assimilation). Second, the majority culture is of higher value than the minority cultures. Third, it is assumed that both majority and minority group members can have a solid grounding in the majority group culture. Through this solid grounding, minority group members eventually become equipped to compete on "level ground" in the mainstream.

These three assumptions underlying the melting-pot hypothesis manifest themselves in various ways, sometimes explicitly. For example, Dr. Tate, the U.K. chief advisor on school curriculums proposed:

> The best guarantee of strong minority cultures is the existence of a majority culture which is sure of itself, which signals that customs and traditions are things to be valued and which respects other cultures.
>
> *The Weekly Telegraph*, August 1, 1995, 210, p. 9

In an article entitled "We should teach all pupils to be British," the conservative English newspaper in which Dr. Tate was quoted went on to report him as having said,

> Children should be taught what it means to be British whatever their cultural or ethnic origins . . . British   c u l t u r e s h o u l d n o t b e compromised to take account of a multi-ethnic Britain. Christianity should be taught to all children and they should all have a good understanding of British history and literature.
>
> *The Weekly Telegraph*, August 1, 1995, 210, p. 9

The report added that Dr. Tate dismissed the ("relativist") view that no set of cultural values should be taught above any others. "From this perspective," said Dr. Tate, "there is no more need to teach Latin than Sanskrit, classical civilization than the history of the American West."

Reassessing the Multicultural Hypothesis and the Assimilation Hypothesis

Inherent in both the multiculturalism and assimilationist hypotheses are assumptions about how changes in culture and in intergroup relations can be controlled in a "top-down" manner by political, economic, and other macro-level processes. These assumptions arise from a "causal" model that has dominated mainstream social science thinking, and particularly psychology. A main goal of psychological research is taken to be the discovery of "causal relations." Consequently, the classic psychological experiment involves manipulations of independent variables (assumed causes) in order to measure their effects on dependent variables (effects). Put in these terms, we can formulate the starting proposition of the multiculturalism and the assimilationist hypotheses as follows: The manipulation of feelings of confidence in own identity (independent variable) causes predictable changes in behavior toward out-group members (dependent variable).

Some Historical Evidence

However, even if we do view the starting assumption of the multiculturalism and assimilation hypotheses from a causal perspective, the evidence bearing on this assumption seems contradictory. For example, when considering historical cases, one could argue that the Nazis were confident in their own identity, but this did not lead them to be open and accepting toward minorities. Similarly, one might point to many other political and religious fundamentalist movements around the world, all of which seem to be confident in their own identities, but at the same time seem determined to implement their own version of "ethnic cleansing" by eliminating particular minorities. Such examples seem to cast doubt on the proposition that confidence in one's own identity leads to acceptance of others.

In response, one could raise the question, "Were Nazis such as Hitler really confident in their own identities?" Many thinkers have responded no to this question. For example, in his insightful analysis of Nazi Germany, Fischer has concluded: "There is almost universal agreement among historians that Hitler was high-strung and habitually anxious about everything. He was a rigid and infantile character who felt himself deeply unworthy and was afflicted by neurotic fears and obsessions" (1995, p. 301).

More generally, one could ask: "Are hate-mongering religious and political fanatics really confident in their own identities, or do they in fact suffer from a lack of confidence?" The idea that such groups lack confidence is supported by the original research on the authoritarian personality (Adorno, Frenkel-Brunswik, Levinson, Sanford, 1950), as well as more recent research on right-wing authoritarianism (Altemeyer, 1981, 1988) and various extremist groups (Billig, 1978). Similarly, research indicates that those high on the personality trait of Machiavellianism have a tendency to feel vulnerable in a world that is potentially hostile (Christie & Geise, 1970), and fascism seems to arise out of fear and weakness in the face of perceived uncertainty and threats, rather than feelings of strength and confidence (Gregor, 1974). While that may be, the important point for policy is the normative character of the regimes, no matter how insecure or neurotic those who originate and promulgate them are. Since adherence to norms is an option, an act or decision, nonadherence is conceived as willful and so is punishable. Hence there is a tendency to define persecution of minorities as a punitive reaction.

Lessons from Historical Cases

The cases of Germany, Japan and Italy during World War II are enough to remind us that education level or even "high culture" per se is not enough to save a society from going down a destructive path. (Of course, even this judgment is a story told from the point of view of the victors. Had the Axis powers won World War II the assumed psychological consequences of a high standard of education would have been quite different.) If we are to take seriously the assumption that education and rationality will prevent the growth of authoritarianism, we must do a better job of identifying the kind of education and rationality that will improve the situation. It is not enough to look back to the Hitlers of the world and "explain" their behavior through reference to a lack of solid education (e.g., "Hitler was a profoundly miseducated man who lacked a solid foundation in any field," Fischer, 1995, p. 303). The same could not have been said of Albert Speer or Heinrich Himmler.

In essence, although the majority of thinkers have used historic examples to argue that prejudiced behavior, authoritarianism, and biased-intergroup behavior generally arise from a lack of confidence, there remains a great deal of ambiguity in this area, particularly since the case has clearly involved selective attention to examples.

Evidence from Laboratory Research

The relationship between motivation and intergroup bias is not made any clearer by experimental laboratory research. If we take self-esteem to be an indicator of "feelings of confidence," the empirical evidence fails to provide a clear picture of the relationship between self-esteem and intergroup behavior (Hogg & Abrams, 1990), despite the fact that this relationship is central to the most important contemporary intergroup theory and has been the focus of empirical investigation since at least the mid 1970s (see Taylor & Moghaddam, 1994, ch. 4).

A number of laboratory studies in which individuals are assigned to groups on the basis of "minimal" criteria suggest that the opportunity to show bias in favor of the in-group and against the out-group leads to elevated self-esteem (Lemyre & Smith, 1985) and a more positive social identity in Tajfelian terms (Oaks & Turner, 1980). However, using the minimal group paradigm, Hogg and Sunderland (1991) found that successful discrimination does not elevate self-esteem, although depressed self-esteem does lead to higher discrimination. Studies using a variety of other experimental procedures show mixed results on the relationship between threats to self-esteem and intergroup discrimination (Brown, Collins & Schmidt, 1988; Crocker, Thompson, McGraw, & Ingerman, 1987; Meindl & Lerner, 1984).

Crocker and Major (1989) pointed to one of the many possible reasons for the complex relationship between self-esteem and discrimination in everyday life. Under certain conditions, ego-threatened individuals may take shelter within an in-group, minimizing their contact with outsiders. Through intra-group social comparisons, biased filtering of self-evaluations, and other self-protective strategies, stigmatized groups may maintain high self-esteem despite being the target of discrimination. Similarly, those who are the source of discrimination may use self-protective strategies to maintain a high self-esteem. Extreme examples of this would be white supremacist groups and militias in North America and Western Europe, who often organize themselves in isolated but cohesive bands.

Social Reducton Theory and Future Directions for Normative Accounts of Motivation

Our focus on social motivation is not intended to highlight assumed "mental mechanisms," such as attitudes or attributions. Rather, it is intended to bring to center stage skilled behavior in everyday social practices. In this endeavor, the insights provided by social reducton theory may prove useful (Moghaddam & Harré, 1995). A social reducton is an elementary practice, implementing a norm and requiring the exercise of a related skill that bears directly on a social relationship. Each social reducton is a correct way of doing something in a particular context, "how to" say goodbye, how to express condolences, and so on. Social reducton theory proposes that social change is structured by social reducton systems, that are interconnected networks for locally valid practices, implemented through norms and related social skills that realize social relationships in particular domains. The implication of this theory is that the behavior of individuals tends to be dependent on contexts and their structures, rather than motivation "inside the self."

For example, consider the case of a long-time smoker who is attempting to quit smoking. He may be persuaded that smoking is a health hazard, and his "attitudes" toward smoking may change - in so far as he is able to express all the "right" sentiments about the ills of smoking. In other words, his "personal motivation" to quit smoking may be very high, as measured by what he says. However, this "change of mind" will not necessarily mean that he will be able to stop smoking in practice. Smokers typically find that they will only be able to quit if, rather than changing "their minds," they can become skilled in following a different set of activities. Thus, by altering the routines of their everyday lives (e.g., no longer sitting around the table after dinner or changing the timetable for work breaks), smokers find it easier to "kick the habit." Such altered everyday social practices embody motivation. Contextual demands are more powerful than any declarations of attitudes.

This social interpretation of motivation better explains why it is so difficult for individuals to quit a certain "life style," such as a criminal one. For example, the United States now has approximately 1.7 million people in its prisons, and one of the "booming" areas of employment for psychologists in the United States is in the prison system. If the purpose of the prison system is to reform individuals and lead them away from crime, it has failed. The main reason for this failure is the individualistic ethos that motivation resides in the person and that those who really want to reform can reform themselves. In practice, most criminals leave the prison system and reenter the same set of social networks that existed for them before they entered prison. In other words, they are only skilled in the "same old" social practices. Their "change of mind" and personal motivation, as expressed in discussions with prison counsellors and psychologists, is soon swept aside by a far more pervasive and powerful source of motivation that resides in the collective life around them. In the final analysis, then, it is culture, "the way things are done here," that is the source of motivation. Indeed, the prison system itself is a context in which evaluation is above all by reference to criminal life itself.

Concluding Comment

Mainstream psychology attempts to explain behavior through references to assumed universal mental mechanisms (Fiske & Taylor, 1991). In line with this approach, researchers studying intergroup conflict have looked inside individuals for causes of collective conflict. A major assumption has been that intergroup conflict can be resolved through influencing motivation inside individuals. However, the empirical evidence does not show a direct causal link between personal motivation and intergroup conflict. Moreover, we propose that the entire causal model should be set aside because human behavior is better explained through normative accounts that assume that persons are intentionally engaged in skilled, rule-following behavior that responds to the demands of context, with its implicit norms and models for correct behavior.

We are not proposing that rules, norms, or culture generally "causes" behavior in a deterministic manner. Rather, each culture provides a normative system that prescribes how things should be done. From this perspective, motivation is embedded in normative systems, and the most important source of motivation is collective life rather than private consciousness.

Critical Thinking Exercises

(1) The tendency to look inside individuals for explanations of social behavior and societal conditions is influenced by American culture. Discuss this statement.
(2) What implication does it have for control if we explain motivation as being social and part of society, rather than personal and inside individuals?

19

Toward Solutions: Performance-Driven Control (PDC) in our Personal and Professional Lives

It is a characteristic of wisdom not to do desperate things.

Henry Thoreau, *Economy, Walden* (1854)

In our efforts to outline solutions in this final chapter, we keep in mind Thoreau's caution to the effect that desperate acts are not wise acts. We have argued that planning in personal and professional domains is often influenced by illusions of control, but it would be a desperate act to see the solution as the abandonment of all planning. Our proposed solution is much wiser, but nonetheless innovative.

We begin by recapping the main thesis of the previous eighteen chapters. This summary acts as a launching pad for our proposed solution, which we entitle Performance-Driven Control (PDP). A major advantage of Performance-Driven Control is that it minimizes the possibility that illusions will influence our plans, and at the same time, maximizes the impact of actual performance and changing conditions on plans.

Illusions of Control: A Recap

Planning is an integral part of all life activities, from the most intimate and personal to those that are public and involve corporate and government organizations. From our earliest years, we are influenced by the plans that others, such as our parents and teachers, make for us, as well as those we develop for ourselves. A child of seven has already become a planner, and is the inheritor of many plans. She plans to build a tree house for herself, at the same time her parents have plans for her to learn to play the piano and to learn foreign languages. In this sense, we could replace Aristotle's famous dictum that "man is a political animal" with the dictum that "man is a planning animal."

Because plans are about the future, they inevitably incorporate assumptions about future conditions and events. Such assumptions include how other people will behave, how market conditions will change, what house prices will be like next year, and so on. A massive body of social science knowledge, including psychological, sociological, anthropological, and economic knowledge, exists to guide us in our efforts to predict the future. A wide variety of social science techniques also exist to help us try to control future events. Efforts to predict and control the future are based on causal models of human behavior, derived from a positivist view of science. These include predicting changes in the stock market, controlling worker productivity, eradicating authoritarianism, and so on. We now know that most events in human societies are not predictable, and that positivism is not a good basis for social science research (nor for research in the physical sciences, but that is beyond the scope of this discussion).

The unpredictability of future events means that planning in the traditional sense does not work well. Conditions change, unpredictable events arise, and in the majority of cases plans have to be revised or completely cast aside. Changes in the economy and other factors mean that the stock market does not behave as we had expected, a strike is called at a factory where we thought worker satisfaction was high, authoritarianism persists in a "liberal" age, market conditions shift so that our "winner" product becomes a loser and we have to change directions to take advantage of an unexpected winner. Everyone with practical experience in making five-year plans knows this to be the case. The question arises, then, as to why so many people continue to make plans in their personal and professional lives.

The answer is that people continue to make plans because they find them useful in some important ways. Plans can help to direct energies and resources, give greater meaning to everyday actions, and generally inspire us to greater effort. They can also give us a sense of being in control of our personal and professional lives. Two examples will illustrate this. The diet plan a woman follows makes her feel more in control of her health, just as the CEO and his team feel safer now they have a five-year plan charting out how the company should progress. Plans can be beneficial and can help enhance our performance in getting tasks done.

Problems arise when illusions of control creep into our lives and dominate how we behave. The gambler imagines that she really can determine how the dice will fall, the father assumes he will determine the happiness of his daughter when she grows up, the manager thinks he can direct the success of new recruits to his company, the university president imagines she can control which research areas will flourish in the future, the CEO believes he has mapped out the future of the corporation for the next five years, and so on. Control in such cases is illusory, and whether plans work out is chance based, in large part because of the fast-paced, changing environment.

The nature of change at the turn of the twenty-first century is shaped more and more by technology that is based on research in increasingly specialized domains. For example, drug development over the next few decades could be dramatically influenced by genetic and bioengineering research. Specialists in narrow lines of research are cut off from researchers in other specialties. This is reflected by the mushrooming of specialized conventions and the disappearance of multidisciplinary events. The techniques, languages, and cultures of each research specialty have become so different that it makes communication with outsiders very difficult. This becomes clear when one looks at the proliferation of specialist journals, now in the thousands, each using its own jargon.

Consequently, it becomes next to impossible for outsiders to understand the details of research in a specialty and to appreciate the potential for such research to have practical consequences. For example, a major pharmaceutical company will have hundreds of research projects, and no one can predict which particular projects will bear fruit and lead to commercially successful drugs. The unpredictability of technological breakthroughs arising from specialized research means that chance plays a very large part in the success of planning. Many different R&D disciplines contribute results over an extended period of time.

When events move in the same direction as our plans, our illusions of control become reinforced. We believe more strongly than ever that we really do have control over events, even though the reasons for a course of events may be very different from what we imagine.

Major problems arise when illusions of control influence us to adhere rigidly to preset plans. As events move in a direction that is different from our plans, we may imagine that we can still redirect events and return to the "correct" path set out in the plan.

Performance-Driven Control (PDC)

Just as people of all walks of life make plans in their personal and professional lives, everyone is also a manager. Some people become employed as professional managers, but all of us are managers in our everyday lives. This is not to imply that we are explicit in our attempts to plan, control, coordinate, and motivate ourselves and others, but rather that we undertake all of these tasks nevertheless. "Everyday life" or amateur managers are just as prone to illusions of control as are professional managers. Thus, the solution we are putting forward is not directed just at those who are professionally employed as managers; it is put forward as a methodology that can be useful to amateur managers as well - the parents managing their family life, the medical doctor managing his practice, the dieter managing her health and food intake, the athlete managing his training.

Performance-Driven Control (PDC) involves striving for a vision through performance-proven, short-term action plans and continuously realigned short-term goals. There are three key elements in this definition.

Vision is made up of a "core ideology" which James Collins and Jerry Porras (1994) have described in *Built to Last* as core values brought together with a purpose. Core values are an organization's essential and enduring tenets. For example, among the core values of visionary companies are "service to the customer above all else" (Nordstrom's), "continuous self-renewal" (Motorola), "product excellence" (Procter & Gamble), "to elevate the Japanese culture and national status" (Sony), "be in partnership with employees" (Wal-Mart), and "to bring happiness to millions and to celebrate, nurture, and promulgate wholesome American values" (Walt Disney). Purpose is an organization's reason for existence above and beyond the bottom line. It is a lofty, morally laudable target to aim for, one that goes beyond the profit motive.

Performance-proven, short-term goals involve practical and feasible action steps toward achieving short-term goals. The practicality and feasibility of these goals is proven on the basis of past performance, according to what has already been shown to be possible. *Continuously realigned short-term goals* are specific targets that are selected, assessed, and revised on the basis of actual performance and what experience has proven to be feasible.

In discussions of short-term goals, the time period involved could be extremely short (a matter of hours or days), or much longer (a matter of years or decades).

Continuity/Discontinuity

If the past and the present are used as indicators, there will arise more and more discontinuities in the future. Technological innovations emerging from increasingly specialized research ensure discontinuities,as individuals and organizations change their behaviors in order to take advantage of, or simply cope with, new technologies. Management strategies must enable us to take maximum advantage of new opportunities to be found in discontinuities, as well as the strengths gained through continuities. Performance-Driven Control achieves this through incorporating a continuous long-term vision, coupled with flexible short-term goals that change with discontinuities. The flexibility of short-term goals and the role of the continuous vision become clear when we consider the four basic phases in the cycle of Performance-Driven Control (see figure 19.1).

The Performance-Driven Management Cycle

Phase One: Performance-Inspiring Vision
To identify a vision that will inspire performance is the first step and the most important challenge facing individuals, organizations, and nations. In order to inspire, a vision must seem attainable, yet also be lofty and noble. This magical balance between the mundane and the sublime, the everyday and the eternal, the earthly and the divine, is difficult to achieve, but all real progress depends upon it for both individuals and groups.

The dieter must have a vision of himself as a slim person and see this as both a wonderful thing to achieve and a practical possibility, or he will not be inspired to keep to his diet. If he has a vision of himself as a slim person, but really does not value being slim, or does not think it a feasible possibility, then he is very unlikely to stick to his diet. Similarly, the entrepreneur and the manager must have visions that are at the same time grand and feasible, or employees will not feel inspired to make the necessary efforts and sacrifices to reach the vision.

Phase Two: Performance-Powered Planning

A vision acts as an inspiration and a guide, but it is a long way away. The ideal slim figure that the dieter has in mind, the national company that the small entrepreneur is thinking about, the "top 3" multinational corporation that the CEO is shooting for, these are all a long way into the future. In order to move toward a vision, there is a need to plan out short-term action steps. These must be concrete and practical. In this sense, the process of planning must be reality based.

We describe planning as "performance controlled" because short-term plans must be based on actual performance capabilities. This is no place for pie-in-the sky schemes. Rather, actual past performance must be assessed in order to make realistic estimates of what is actually feasible. How many pounds did the dieter actually lose over the last six months of dieting? How much growth has the small company achieved since it was started five years ago? How much of the international market share has the would-be multinational corporation taken over during the last few years? A hard and critical look at past performance allows for realistic short-term plans to be mapped out.

Phase Three: Performance-Directed Action

Action is now taken to implement short-term goals. The objective is to achieve short-term goals. This is because it is only through improved performance on achieving short-term goals that real progress is made toward the adopted vision. If the dieter can lose four pounds a month, chances are very good that he can lose all the twenty pounds he needs to lose in six months. If productivity rises by 10 percent in the first twelve weeks, the CEO is likely to reach the goal of achieving a 25 percent increase in five years.

Short-term goals are flexible and have to be changed to better exploit new opportunities, which are also discontinuities. For example, if a new, safe, and effective "weight-reducing pill" comes onto the market, the dieter might change short-term goals (he might say, for instance, "This month I will not lose any weight, because I will slowly switch to using the new pill. But I will lose six pounds during each of the three months after that"). The CEO might decide that for the next year, the main priority of the company must be to shift production to take advantage of a new technological breakthrough. Although productivity will not go up during this changeover, after that it will go up 15 percent a year.

Short-term goals change with discontinuities associated with fast-changing technologies, market conditions, and the like, but they are always directed toward achieving a vision that is continuous and long term.

Phase Four: Performance Control Process

Performance needs to be continuously monitored. This is essential not only to quickly identify shortcomings in performance, but also to maintain a realistic basis for plans. The development of short-term plans toward the long-term vision must be tied closely and directly to actual performance, and not some imaginary idea of how performance should or could be going.

It is difficult to overstate the importance of this phase, because its neglect will lead to illusions of control. If performance is not monitored accurately, plans will be made on the basis of inaccurate estimates of what can be accomplished. Rifts will arise between plans and actual performance. Consequently, plans will relate to a hypothetical world, while actual events move in a different direction. Such plans can only enable managers to enjoy control in an illusory manner.

Performance-Driven Control is cyclical; the four phases are overlapping, and each phase can lead back to any of the previous phases.

Concluding Comment

Illusions of control seem to be an inevitable part of the human experience; they have both positive and negative consequences. Our argument has been that illusions of control are generally underestimated, or even completely overlooked. This has resulted in their negative consequences also being overlooked. We have put forward a modest proposal for minimizing illusions of control when they can have negative consequences. It would be foolish to try to end illusions of control completely, for the simple reason that assuming ourselves to be in control often makes us feel better.

Bibliography

Abramson, L. Y. (Ed.). (1988). *Social cognition and clinical psychology*. New York: Guilford Press.

Adorno, T. W., Frenkel-Brunswik, E., Levinson, D. J., & Sanford, R. W. (1950). *The authoritarian personality*. New York: Harper & Row.

Alderfer, C. P. (1972). *Existence, relatedness, and growth*. New York: Free Press.

Allport, G. W. (1954). *The nature of prejudice*. Cambridge, MA: Addison-Wesley.

Altemeyer, B. (1981). *Right-wing authoritarianism*. Winnipeg: University of Manitoba.

_____ (1988). *Enemies of freedom: Understanding right-wing authoritarianism*. San Fransisco: Jossey-Bass.

Bell, P. A., Fisher, J. D., Baum, A., & Greene, T. E. (1990), *Environmental psychology* (3rd ed.). Fort Worth, TX: Holt, Rinehart and Winston.

Billig, M. (1978). *Fascists: A social psychological view of the National Front*. London: Academic Press.

Bloom, A. (1987). *The closing of the American mind*. New York: Simon & Schuster.

Borel, J. F., & Kis, Z. L. (1991). The discovery and development of Cyclosporine (Sandimmune), *Transplantation Proceedings, 23*, 1867-1874.

Bounds, G., Yorks, L., Adams, M., & Ranney, G. (1994). *Beyond total quality management: Toward the emerging paradigm*. New York: McGraw-Hill.

Bowles, J., & Hammond, J. (1991). *Beyond quality: New standards of total performance that can change the future of corporate America*. New York: Berkeley.

Bowser, B. P. (Ed.) (1995). *Racism and antiracism in world perspective*. Thousand Oaks, CA: Sage.

Brown, D. E. (1991). *Human universals*. Philadelphia: Temple University Press.

Brown, J. D., Collins, R. L., & Schmidt, G. W. (1988). Self-esteem and direct versus indirect forms of self-enhancement. *Journal of Personality and Social Psychology, 55*, 445-453.

Buss, D. M. (1994). *The evolution of desire: Strategies of human mating.* New York: Basic Books.

Carrol, L. (1965). *Alice's adventures in wonderland & Through the looking glass.* New York: Airmont. (Original work published 1865)

Chagnon, N. A. (1988). Life histories, blood revenge, and warfare in a tribal population. *Science, 239*, 985-992.

_____ (1992). *Yanomamo.* (4th ed.) New York: Harcourt Brace Jovanovich.

Champy, J. (1995). *Reengineering management.* New York: Harper.

Chemers, M. M., Oskamp, S., & Costanzo, M. A. (Eds.). (1995). *Diversity in organizations.* Thousand Oaks, CA: Sage.

Christie, R., & Geise, F. L. (1970). *Studies in Machiavellianism.* New York: Academic Press.

Colby, A., Kohlberg, L., Gibbs, J., & Lieberman, M. (1983). A longitudinal study of moral development. *Monographs of the Society for Research in Child Development, 48*, (1-2, Serial No. 200).

Cole, M., & Cole, S. R. (1993). *The development of children.* (2nd ed.). New York: Freeman.

Collins, J. C., & Porras, J. I. (1994). *Built to last: Successful habits of visionary companies.* London: Century.

Crevecoeur, M. G. J. de (1985). Letters from an American farmer. In G. McMichael (Ed.), *Anthology of American literature* (pp. 392-406). New York: Macmillan. (Original work published 1782)

Crocker, J., & Major, B. (1989). Social stigma and self-esteem: The self-protective properties of stigma. *Psychological Review, 96*, 608-630.

Crocker, J., Thompson, L. L., McGraw, K. M., & Ingerman, C. (1987). Downward comparison, prejudice, and evaluation of others: Effects of self-esteem and threat. *Journal of Personality and Social Psychology, 52*, 907-916.

Crosby, P. B. (1996). *Quality is still free.* New York: McGraw-Hill.

Cross, G. (1994). *A social history of leisure.* State College, PA: Venture.

Daley, M., & Wilson, M. (1988). *Homicide.* New York: Aldine de Gruyter.

Dawkins, R. (1976). *The selfish gene.* New York: Oxford University Press.

Deal, T. E., & Kennedy, A. A. (1982). *Corporate culture: The rites and rituals of corporate life.* Reading, MA: Addison-Wesley.

Dennett, D. C. (1995). *Darwin's dangerous idea: Evolution and the meaning of life.* New York: Simon & Schuster.

Deutsch, M. (1993). Educating for a peaceful world. *American psychologist, 48*, 510-517.

Devine, P. G. (1995). Prejudice and out-group perception. In A. Tesser (Ed.), *Advanced social psychology* (pp. 467-524). New York: McGraw-Hill.

Drucker, P. F. (1954). *The practice of management*. New York: Harper & Row.

Drucker, P. F. (1987). *The frontiers of management*. New York: Heiemann.

_____ (1989). *The new realities: In government and politics/In economics and business/In society and worldview*. New York: Harper & Row.

Dye, T. R., & Zeigler, L. H. (1970). *The irony of democracy: An uncommon introduction to American politics*. Belmont, CA.: Wadsworth.

Ellickson, R. C. (1991). *Order without law: How neighbors settle disputes*. Cambridge, MA: Harvard University Press.

Elmer, N. P. (1983). Morality and politics: The ideological dimension in the theory of moral development. In H. Weinreich-Haste & D. Locke (Eds.), *Morality in the making: Thought, action and social context* (pp. 47-71). Chichester: Wiley.

Elmer, N. P., & Hogan, R. (1981). Developing attitudes to law and justice: An integrative view. In S. S. Brehm, S. M. Kassin, & F. X. Gibbons (Eds.), *Developmental social psychology* (pp. 298-314). New York: Oxford University Press.

Elmer, N. P., Renwick, S., & Malone, B. (1983). The relationship between moral reasoning and political orientation. *Journal of Personality and Social Psychology, 45*, 1073-1080.

Field, D. (1981). Can preschool children really learn to conserve? *Child Development, 52*, 326-334.

Fielder, F. E. (1967). *A theory of leadership effectiveness*. New York: McGraw-Hill.

_____ (1987). *New approaches to effective leadership: Cognitive resources and organizational performance*. New York: Wiley.

Fielder, F. E., & Garcia, J. E. (1987). *Leadership: Cognitive resources and performance*. New York: Wiley.

Fischer, K. P. (1995). *Nazi Germany: A new history*. New York: Continuum.

Fisher, R. (1989). *The social psychology of intergroup relations and international conflict resolution*. New York: Springer.

Fiske, S. T., & Taylor, S. E. (1991). *Social cognition* (2nd ed.). New York: McGraw-Hill.

Flavell, J. H. (1963). *The developmental psychology of Jean Piaget*. Princeton, NJ: Van Nostrand.

Freud, S. (1921). Group psychology and the analysis of the ego. In J. Strachey (Ed. & Trans.), *The standard edition of the complete works of Sigmund Freud*. London: Hogarth press.

Friedman, J. W. (1990). *Game theory, with applications to economics*. New York: Oxford University Press.

Friedman, M. (1962). *Capitalism and freedom*. Chicago: University of Chicago Press.

Frost, P. J., & Moore, L. (Eds.). (1991). *Reframing organizational culture*. Thousand Oaks, CA: Sage.

Gaines, S. O., Jr., & Reed, E. S. (1995). Prejudice: From Allport to DuBois. *American Psychologist, 50,* 96-103.

Galbraith, J. K. (1994). *A journey through economic time: A firsthand view.* New York: Houghton Mifflin.

George, S., & Weimerskirch, A. (1994). *Total quality management: Techniques proven at today's most successful companies.* New York: Wiley.

Goffman, E. (1963). *Stigma: Notes on the management of spoiled identity.* Englewood Cliffs, NJ: Prentice Hall.

Gregor, J. A. (1974). *Interpretations of fascism.* Morristown, N. J.: General Learning Press.

Grimsley, K. D. (1996, May 26). Why men stay silent: Fear of retaliation fostered abusive atmosphere, Mitsubishi workers say. *Washington Post,* pp. H1, H7.

Hammer, M., & Champy, J. (1993). *Reengineering the corporation.* New York: Harper Business.

Harré, R. (1984). *Personal being.* Cambridge, MA: Harvard University Press.
_____ (1994). *Social being* (2nd ed.). Oxford: Blackwell.

Hart, C. W. M., Pilling, A. R., & Goodale, J. C. (1988). *The Tiwi of North Australia.* (3rd ed.) New York: Holt, Rinehart & Winston, Inc.

Hayne, H., Rovee-Collier, C., & Perris, E. E. (1987). Categorization and memory retreival by three-month-olds. *Child Development, 58,* 750-767.

Hayward, S. F. (1997). *Churchill on leadership: Executive success in the face of adversity.* Rocklin, CA.: Prima Publishing.

Hearnshaw, L. S. (1987). *A History of Western psychology.*

Henslin, M. (1967). Craps and magic. *American Journal of Sociology, 73,* 316-330.

Hirschman, A. O. (1984). *Getting ahead collectively: Grassroots experiences in Latin America.* New York: Pergamon.

Hofstede, G. (1980). *Culture's consequences.* Beverly Hills, CA: Sage.

Hogan, R., Curphy, G. J., & Hogan, J. (1994). What we know about leadership: Effectiveness and personality. *American Psychologist, 49,* 493-504.

Hogg, M. A., & Abrams, D. (1990). Social motivation, self-esteem, and social identity. In D. Abrams & M. A. Hogg (Eds.), *Social identity theory: Constructive and critical advances* (pp. 28-47). London: Harvester Wheatsheaf.

Hogg, M. A., & Sunderland, J. (1991). Self-esteem and intergroup discrimination in the minimal group paradigm. *British Journal of Social Psychology, 30,* 51-62.

Holiday, A. (1988). *Moral powers: Normative necessity in language and history.* London: Routledge.

Holmes, S. (1993). *The anatomy of antiliberalism.* Cambridge, MA: Harvard University Press.

Hradesky, J. L. (1995). *Total quality management handbook.* New York: McGraw-Hill.

Hunnicutt, B. K. (1988). *Work without end.* Philadelphia: Temple University Press.

Hunt, J. G. (1991). *Leadership: A new synthesis.* Thousand Oaks, CA: Sage.

Iacocca, L. (1984). *Iacocca.* New York: Bantam.

Inhelder, B., & Piaget, J. (1958). *The growth of logical thinking from childhood to adolescence.* New York: Basic Books.

_____ (1964). *The early growth of logic in the child.* New York: Harper & Row.

Janis, I. L. (1972). *Victims of groupthink: A psychological study of foreign-policy decisions and fiascoes.* Boston: Houghton Mifflin.

_____ (1982). *Groupthink* (2nd ed.). Boston: Houghton Mifflin.

Juran, J. M., & Gryna, F. M. (Eds.). (1988). *Juran's quality control handbook* (4th ed.). New York: McGraw-Hill.

Kanter, R. M. (1989). *When giants learn to dance: Mastering the challenges of strategy, management, and careers in the 1990s.* London: Simon & Schuster.

Kanungo, R. N., & Conger, J. A. (1989). *Charismatic leadership: A behavioral theory and its cross-cultural implications.* Paper presented at the 2nd Regional Conference of the International Association of Cross-Cultural Psychology, Amsterdam.

Keynes, J. M. (1963). The end of laissez faire. In *Essays in persuasion.* New York: Norton.

Kirkpatrick, S. A., & Locke, E. A. (1991). Leadership: Do traits matter? *Academy of Management Executive, 5,* 48-60.

Kohlberg, L. (1984). *The psychology of moral development: The nature and validity of moral stages.* San Fransisco: Harper & Row.

Kouzes, J. M., & Posner, B. Z. (1995). *The leadership challenge.* San Fransisco, CA: Jossey-Bass.

Krugman, P. (1990). *The age of diminished expectations.* Cambridge, MA: MIT Press.

Lambert, W. E., Mermegis, L., & Taylor, D. M. (1986). Greek Canadians' attitudes towards own group and other Canadian ethnic groups: A test of the multicultural hypothesis. *Canadian Journal of Behavioral Science, 18,* 35-51.

Lambert, W. E., & Taylor, D. M. (1990). *Coping with cultural and racial diversity in urban America.* New York: Praeger.

Langer, E. J. (1977). The psychology of chance. *Journal for the theory of social behavior, 7,* 185-208.

Lemyre, R. A., & Smith, P. M. (1985). Intergroup discrimination and self-esteem in the minimal group paradigm. *Journal of Personality and Social Psychology, 49,* 660-670.

Linder, W. (1994). *Swiss democracy: Possible solutions to conflict in multicultural societies.* New York: St. Martin's Press.

Logue, A. W. (1991). *The psychlogy of eating and drinking: An introduction.* (2nd ed.). New York: Freeman.

Lorenz, K. (1966). *On aggression* (M. Wilson, Trans.). New York: Harcourt Brace & Jovanonich.

Lott, B., & Maluso, D. (Eds.). (1995). *The social psychology of interpersonal discrimination.* New York: Guildford Press.

Machaivelli, N. (1961). *The prince.* (G. Bull Trans.). Harmondsworth, UK.: Penguin (first English translation appeared 1640).

MacLegan, P., & Nel, C. (1997). *The age of participation: New governance for the workplace and the world.* San Fransisco, CA: Berrett-Koehler Publishers.

Macnamara, J., & Austin, G. (1993). Physics and plasticine. *Canadian Psychology, 34,* 225-232.

Markovits, H. (1993). Piaget and plasticine: Who's right about conservation? *Canadian Psychologist, 34,* 233-239.

Markus, H. R., & Kitayama, S. (1991). Culture and the self: Implications for cognition, emotion, and motivation. *Psychological Review, 98,* 224-253.

Marx, K. (1979). The eighteenth brumaire of Louis Bonaparte. In *Collected Works* (Vol.11, pp.99-197). London: Lawrence and Wishart. (Original work published 1852)

Maslow, A. (1970). *Motivation and personality* (2nd ed.). New York: Harper & Row.

Mayr, E. (1982). *The growth of biological thought.* Cambridge, MA: Belknap Press of Harvard University Press.

McCarthy, J. D., & Zald, M. N. (1977). Resource mobilization and social movements: A partial theory. *American Journal of Sociology, 82,* 1212-1241.

McInerney, F., & White, S. (1995). *The total quality corporation: How 10 major companies turned quality and environmental challenges to competitive advantage in the 1990's.* New York: Truman.

Meindl, J. R., & Lerner, M. J. (1984). Exacerbation of extreme responses to an outgroup. *Journal of Personality and Social Psychology, 47,* 71-84.

Mileham, P., & Spacie, K. (1996). *Transforming corporate leadership.* London, UK: Pitman.

Miller, D. T., & Ross, M. (1975). Self-serving biases in the attribution of causality: Fact or fiction? *Psychological Bulletin, 82,* 213-225.

Moghaddam, F. M. (1990). Modulative and generative orientations in psychology: Implications for psychology in the three worlds. *Journal of Social Issues, 46,* 21-41.

_____ (1992). Assimilation et multiculturalisme: Le cas des minorités au Québec. *Review québécoise de psychologie, 13,* 140-157.

_____ (1993). Managing cultural diversity: North American experiences and suggestions for the German unification process. *International Journal of Psychology, 28,* 727-741.

_____ (1997). *The specialized society: The plight of the individual in an age of individualism.* New York: Praeger.

_____ (1998). *Social psychology: Exploring universals across cultures.* New York: Freeman.

Moghaddam, F. M., & Crystal, D. (1997). Revolutions, Samurai, and reductons: Change and continuity in Iran and Japan. *Journal of Political Psychology, 18,* 355-384.

Moghaddam, F. M., & Harré, R. (1992). Rethinking the laboratory experiment. *American Behavioral Scientist, 36,* 22-38.

_____ (1995). But is it science? Traditional and alternative approaches to the study of social behavior. *World Psychology, 1,* 47-78.

_____ (1996). Psychological limits to political revolution: An application of social reducton theory. In E. Hasselberg, L. Martienssen & F. Radtke (Eds.), *The concept of dialogue at the end of the 20th century* (pp. 230-240). Berlin, Germany: Hegel Institute.

Moghaddam, F. M., & Solliday, E. A. (1991). Balanced multiculturalism and the challenge of peaceful coexistence in pluralistic societies. *Psychology and Developing Societies, 3,* 51-72.

Moghaddam, F.M., & Studer, C. (1997). Cross-cultural psychology: The frustrated gadfly's promises, potentialities, and failures. In D. Fox & I. Prilleltensky (eds.), *Critical psychology: An introduction* (pp. 185-201). Thousand Oaks, CA.: Sage.

Moghaddam, F. M., Taylor, D. M., Lambert, W. E., & Schmidt, A. E. (1995). Attributions and discrimination: A study of attributions to the self, the group, and external factors among whites, blacks, and Cubans in Miami. *Journal of Cross-Cultural Psychology, 26,* 209-220.

Moghaddam, F. M., Taylor, D. M., & Wright, S. C. (1993). *Social psychology in cross-cultural perspective.* New York: Freeman.

Moghaddam, F. M., & Vuksanovic, V. (1990). Attitudes and behavior toward human rights across different contexts: The role of right-wing authoritarianism, political ideology, and religiosity. *International Journal of Psychology, 25,* 455-474.

Newman, C. (1988). *Fall from grace: The experience of downward mobility in the American middle class.* New York: Free Press.

Niemira, M. P., & Klein, P. A. (1994). *Forecasting financial and economic cycles.* New York: John Wiley.

Northouse, P. (1997). *Leadership: Theory and practice.* Thousand Oaks, CA: Sage.

Ormerod, P. (1994). *The death of economics.* London: Faber & Faber.

Ostaszewski, A. (1993). *Mathematics in economics: Models and methods.* Oxford: Blackwell.

Ott, J. S. (1989). *The organizational culture perspective.* Pacific Grove, CA: Brooks/Cole.

Ouchi, W. (1981). *Theory Z: How American business can meet the Japanese challenge.* Reading, Mass.: Addison-Wesley.

Pareto, V. (1935). *The mind and society* (4 Vols.). New York: Dover.

Parker, D., & Stacey, R. (Eds.). (1994). *Chaos, management, and economics: The implications of non-linear thinking.* London: Institute of Economic Affairs.

Parrott, W. G. (1993). Beyond hedonism: Motives for inhibiting or maintaining good and bad moods. In D. M. Wegner & J. W. Pennebaker (Eds.), *Handbook of mental control* (pp. 278-305). Englewood Clifs, NJ: Prentice Hall.

Pincus, J. D., & De Bonis, J. N. (1994). *Top dog.* New York: McGraw-Hill.

Plato. (1987). *The republic* (Desmond Lee, Trans.). Harmondsworth,UK: Penguin.

Poor, R. (1970). *4 days, 40 hours: Reporting a revolution in work and leisure.* Cambridge: Bursk & Poor.

Robinson, D. N. (1995). *An intellectual history of psychology* (3rd ed.). Madison: University of Wisconsin Press.

Rogers, C. (1961). *On becoming a person.* Boston: Houghton Mifflin.

Ross, M., & Sicoly, F. (1979). Egocentric biases in availability and attribution. *Journal of Personality and Social Psychology, 37,* 322-336.

Salisbury, H. E. (1992). *The new emperors: China in the era of Mao and Deng.* New York: Avon.

Samuelson, P. A., & Nordhaus, W. A. (1992). *Economics* (14th ed.). New York: McGraw-Hill.

Schein, E. H. (1985). *Organizational culture and leadership.* San Fransisco, CA: Jossey-Bass.

_____(1992). *Organizational culture and leadership* (2nd ed.). San Francisco, CA: Jossey-Bass.

Seligman, M. E. P. (1991). *Learned optimism.* New York: Knopf.

Shor, J. B. (1992). *The overworked American.* New York: Basic Books.

Sidanius, J., Pratto, F., & Bobo, L. (1994). Social dominance orientation and the political psychology of gender: A case of invariance? *Journal of Personality and Social Psychology, 67,* 998-1011.

Siegel, L. S. (1993). Amazing new discovery: Piaget was wrong! *Canadian Psychology, 34,* 239-245.

Siegler, R. (1995). *Nothing is; everything becomes: Recent advances in understanding cognitive-developmental change.* Paper presented at the Biennial Meeting of the Society for Research in Child Development, Indianapolis, Indiana.

Simonton, D. K. (1994). *Greatness: Who makes history and why.* New York: Guildford.

Skinner, B. F. (1938). *The behavior of organisms.* New York: Appleton-Century-Crofts.

_____ (1948). *Walden Two*. New York: Macmillan.

_____ (1971). *Beyond freedom and dignity*. New York: Knopf.

Smith, A. (1976). *An inquiry into the nature and causes of the wealth of nations.* (Vols. 1 and 2). R. H. Campbell and A. S. Skinner (Eds.). London: Oxford at the Clarendon Press. (Original work published 1776)

Starkey, D. (1981). The origins of concept formation: Object sorting and object preference in early infancy. *Child Development, 52*, 489-497.

Stevenson, W. B., & Gilly, M. C. (1991). Information processing and problem solving: The migration of problems through formal positions and networks of ties. *Academy of Management Journal, 34*, 918-928.

Stover, E., & Nightingale, E. O. (Eds.) (1985). *The breaking of bodies and minds.* New York: Freeman.

Sugerman, S. (1983). *Children's early thought.* Cambridge: Cambridge University Press.

Sumner, W. R. (1906). *Folkways*. Boston: Ginn.

Swift, J. (1960). *Gulliver's travels*. Boston: Houghton Mifflin. (Original work published 1726)

Tajfel, H. (1978). Social categorization, social identity, and social comparison. In H. Tajfel (Ed.), *Differentiation between social groups* (pp. 61-76). London: Academic Press.

Tajfel, H. (Ed.) (1982). *Social identity and intergroup relations.* Cambridge: Cambridge University Press.

Tajfel, H., & Turner, J. C. (1979). An integrative theory of intergroup conflict. In W. G. Austin & S. Worchel (Eds.), *The social psychology of intergroup relations* (pp. 33-47). Monterey, CA.: Brooks/Cole.

Tan, S. L., & Moghaddam, F. M. (1995). Reflexive positioning and culture. *Journal for the Theory of Social Behavior, 25*, 387-400.

Taylor, D. M. (1991). The social psychology of racial and cultural diversity: Issues of assimilation and multiculturalism. In A. Reynolds (Ed.), *Bilingualism, multiculturalism, and second language learning* (pp. 1-19). Hillsdale,NJ: Lawrence Erlbaum.

Taylor, D. M., & Moghaddam, F. M. (1987). *Theories of intergroup relations: International social psychological perspectives.* New York: Praeger.

_____ (1994). *Theories of intergroup relations* (2nd ed.). Westport, CT: Praeger.

Taylor, F. D. (1964). *The principles of scientific management.* New York: Harper & Row. (Original work published 1911)

Taylor, S. E. (1989). *Positive illusions*. New York: Basic Books.

Thatcher, M. (1993). *The Downing Street years.* New York: HarperCollins.

Thomas, B. (1995). *The human dimension of quality.* New York: McGraw-Hill.

Tocqueville, Alexis de (1845). *Democracy in America* (H. Reeve, Trans.). New York: Henry G. Langley.

Van den Berghe, P. (1987). *The ethnic phenomenon.* New York: Praeger.

Vroom, V. H. (1960). *Some personality determinants of the effects of participation*. Englewood Cliffs, NJ: Prentice-Hall.

Vroom, V. H., & Jago, A. G. (1988). *The new leadership: Managing participation in organizations*. Englewood Cliffs, N.J.: Prentice Hall.

Wagner III, J. A., & Hollenback, J. R. (1992). *Management of organizational behavior*. Englewood Cliffs, N.J.: Prentice Hall.

Watson, J. B. (1930). *Behaviorism* (Rev. ed.). New York: Norton.

Weber, M. (1947). *The theory of social and economic organization*. New York: Free Press.

Wetherell, M. (1982). Cross-cultural studies of minimal groups: Implications for social identity theory and intergroup relations. In H. Tajfel (Ed.), *Social identity and intergroup relations*. Cambridge: Cambridge University Press.

Worley, J. A. (1995, May 29). In *Time*.

Yang, M. M. (1994). *Gifts, favors, and banquets: The art of social relationships in China*. Ithaca, NY: Cornell University.

Zald, M. N., & McCarthy, J. D. (1987). *Social movements in an organizational society*. New Brunswick, NJ: Transaction.

Subject Index

Name Index

About the Authors

FATHALI M. MOGHADDAM is Professor of Psychology at Georgetown University in Washington, D.C. and is the co-author of *Theories of Intergroup Relations* (Praeger, 1994).

CHARLES STUDER is a management practitioner in Switzerland.

ISBN 0-275-96025-0

90000>

EAN

9 780275 960254

HARDCOVER BAR CODE